MW01704991

Graphic Design:

A Career Guide and Education Directory

Edited by Sharon Helmer Poggenpohl

AIGA Press New York

This publication was underwritten in part by a grant from the National Endowment for the Arts.

The AIGA would like to thank Potlatch Corporation for its generous contribution of *Quintessence Remarque Velvet* 50/10 recycled paper for the publication of this volume.

Design and Production by Ligature Inc., Boston, Massachusetts.

The AIGA would like to thank Eastern Rainbow, Inc. for its contribution toward separations and film, and Reynolds DeWalt Printing, Inc. for its contribution toward the printing and binding of this volume.

Printed and bound in the United States of America.
ISBN: 1-884081-00-2

Foreword

This guide is intended to help individuals make decisions about preparing for a career in graphic design. It defines the purpose and practice of the field and identifies the strong links between effective educational programs and effective professional practice. Suggestions are made to help the individual evaluate schools as well as potential employers, and comments from educators and practitioners provide insight into their expectations when evaluating prospective students and employees. In addition, noteworthy projects are presented to give the reader a specific sense of the depth and breadth of the field.

Education, at its best, does not simply focus on a career. It provides an opportunity to participate in a community of the mind, to broaden one's perspective and understanding through a variety of studies, and to become acquainted with the pleasure to be gained through the study and practice of graphic design as a discipline, profession, and cultural force. The AIGA was founded for the intellectual profit of its members eighty years ago, a purpose that is central to our programs today and is the primary impetus for the publication of this guide.

We would like to thank Doug Wadden, who had the foresight to initiate this project; the educators and designers whose work and advice add specificity to the guidance given here; Sharon Helmer Poggenpohl, editor, who brought clarity to complexity; Jorge Frascara, Robert O. Swinehart, and Tom Ockerse, who contributed and consulted; Anthony Russell, Gordon Salchow, and Natalia Ilyin for their support and expertise; and the staff of Ligature for their skills in bringing this publication to its ultimate conclusion.

Caroline Hightower
Director

DON'T GET EMOTIONAL. WE'LL BE OPEN SOMETIME IN THE NEAR FUTURE.
M

What is graphic design?

Suppose you want to announce or sell something, amuse or persuade someone, explain a complicated system or demonstrate a process. In other words, you have a message you want to communicate. How do you "send" it? You could tell people one by one or broadcast by radio or loudspeaker. That's verbal communication. But if you use any visual medium at all—if you make a poster; type a letter; create a business logo, a magazine ad, or an album cover; even make a computer printout—you are using a form of **visual communication** called graphic design.

Graphic designers work with drawn, painted, photographed, or computer-generated **images** (pictures), but they also design the **letterforms** that make up various typefaces found in movie credits and TV ads; in books, magazines, and menus; and even on computer screens. Graphic designers create, choose, and organize these elements—typography, images, and the so-called "white space" around them—to communicate a message. Looking at the examples on the following pages will help you recognize how much graphic design is a part of your daily life. From humble things like gum wrappers to huge things like billboards to the T-shirt you're wearing, graphic design informs, persuades, organizes, stimulates, locates, identifies, attracts attention, and provides pleasure.

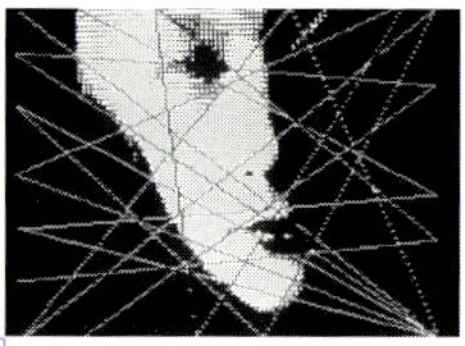

Graphic design is a creative process that combines **art** and **technology** to communicate ideas. The graphic designer works with a variety of communication tools in order to convey a **message** from a client to a particular audience. The main tools are image and typography. Throughout this chapter you will see the work of professional graphic designers, in the larger images, as well as projects created by student designers, in the smaller reproductions. Who are the clients? They are organizations, corporations, and individuals with a message they want to communicate to a specific audience.

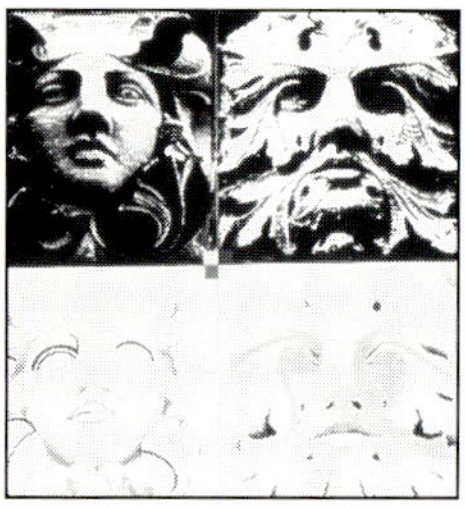

Image-based Design

Graphic designers develop images to represent the ideas their clients want to communicate. Images can be

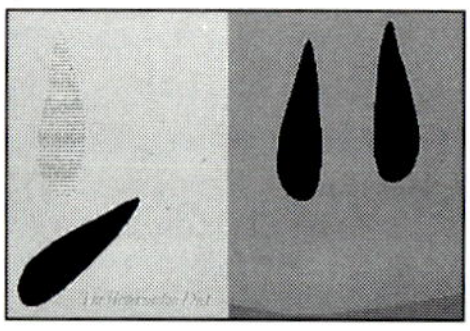

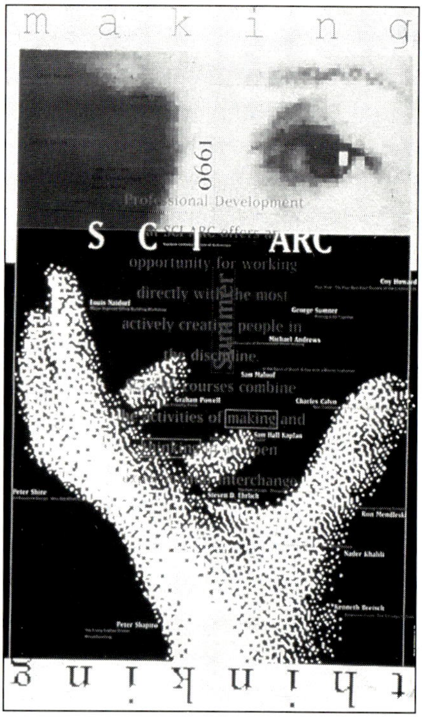

incredibly **powerful** and compelling tools of communication, conveying not only information but also moods and emotions. People respond to images instinctively based on their personalities, associations, and previous experience. For example, you know that a chili pepper is hot, and this knowledge in combination with the image creates a visual pun.

In the case of image-based design, the images must carry the entire message; there are few if any words to help. These images may be photographic, painted, drawn, or graphically rendered in many different ways. Image-based design is employed when the designer determines that, in a particular case, a picture is indeed worth a thousand words.

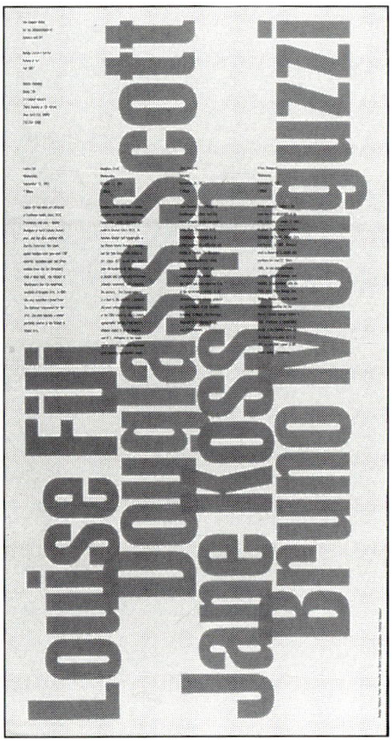

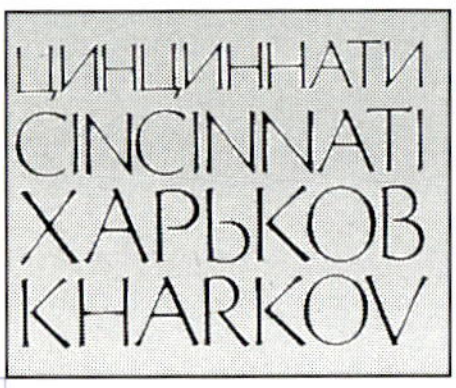

Type-based Design

In some cases, graphic designers rely on words to convey a message, but they use words differently from the ways writers do. To designers, what the words look like is as important as their meaning. The visual forms, whether **typography** (communication designed by means of the printed word) or handmade lettering, perform many communication functions. They can arrest your attention on a poster, identify the product name on a package or a truck, and present running text as the typography in this book does. Graphic designers are experts at presenting information in a visual form in print or on film, packaging, or signs.

When you look at the graphics on this page, it's easy to see what the designer has done. The words look unusual, out of the ordinary. But what about the "ordinary"

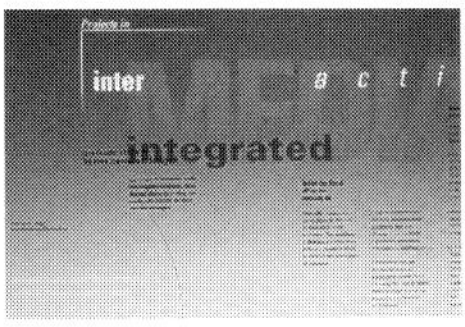

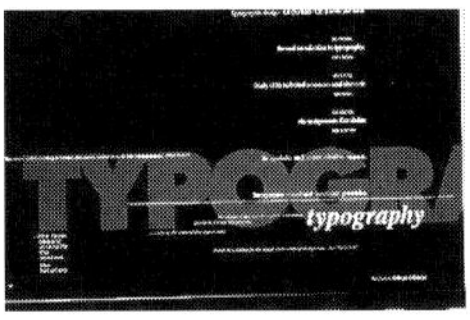

printed page of **running text**? What is involved in designing such a seemingly simple page? To get an idea, turn to page 7. Think about what you would do if you were asked to redesign the page. Would you change the typeface or type size? Would you divide the text into two narrower columns? What about the margins and the spacing between paragraphs and lines? Would you indent the paragraphs or begin them with decorative lettering? What other kinds of treatment might you give the page number? Would you change the boldface terms, perhaps using italic or underlining? What other changes might you consider, and how would they affect the way the reader reacts to the content? Graphic designers evaluate the message and the audience for type-based design in order to make these kinds of decisions—just as the designer of this book did.

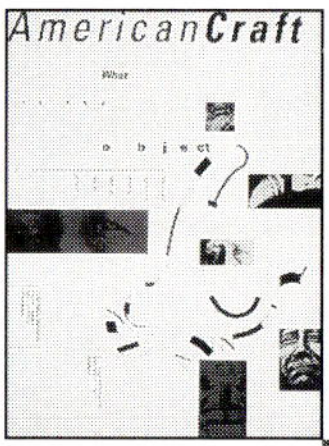

Image and Type

Graphic designers often **combine** images and typography to communicate a client's message to an audience. They explore the creative possibilities presented by words (typography) and images (photography, illustration, and fine art). It is up to the designer not only to find or create appropriate letterforms and images but also to establish the best **balance** between them.

Graphic designers are the link between the client and the audience. On the one hand, a client is often too close to the message to understand the various ways in which it can be presented. The audience, on the other hand, is

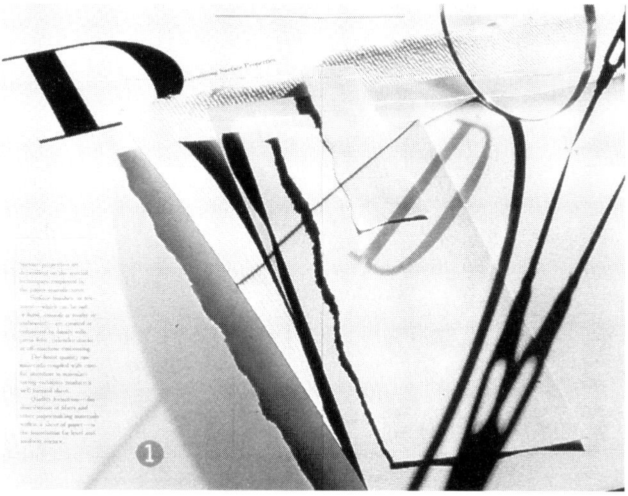

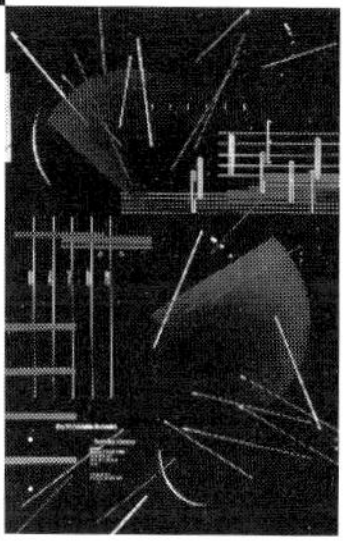

often too broad to have any direct impact on how a communication is presented. What's more, it is usually difficult to make the audience a part of the creative process. Unlike client and audience, graphic designers learn how to construct a message and how to present it successfully. They work with the client to understand the content and the purpose of the message. They often **collaborate** with market researchers and other specialists to understand the nature of the audience. Once a design concept is chosen, the graphic designers work with illustrators and photographers as well as with typesetters and printers or other production specialists to create the final design product.

Symbols, Logos, and Logotypes

Symbols and logos are special, highly condensed information forms or **identifiers.** Symbols are abstract representations of a particular idea or identity. The CBS "eye" and the active "television" are symbolic forms, which we learn to recognize as representing a particular concept or company. Logotypes are corporate identifications based on a special typographical word treatment, as illustrated by the "Connect" example. Some identifiers are hybrid, or combinations of symbol and logotype, such as the rendition of the IBM logo above. In order to create these identifiers, the designer must have a clear vision of the corporation or idea to be

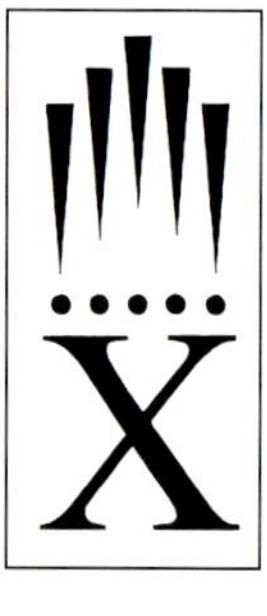

represented and of the audience to which the message is directed.

Let's return to the original question: What is graphic design? This book is an example of graphic design. The words and images on these pages are a **carefully crafted message** from a client, the American Institute of Graphic Arts, to you, a person interested in design as a possible career. Consider how the order of the information and the character of the words and images inform you. There is a designer behind each word and image, thinking about the audience—you—and what your questions and concerns might be.

lecture
the
balance
between
total control
and
total
freedom
presented as part of
Inspiration of Chance
lecture series
with John Cage
friday July 25
cage
The first lecture
balance
between
total control
total
freedom
Inspiration of Chance
lecture series
John Cage
friday July 25
cage

What graphic designers need to know

Graphic designers need to master a wide variety of **skills** and **concepts.** What follows is an overview of the nine categories of investigation you can find in most graphic design programs. They are illustrated with student work. Not every category is taught in every undergraduate curriculum—the time is just too short. Each program emphasizes certain subjects and teaches others more broadly.

Chapter 8 shows different ways to practice graphic design and serves as a counterpoint to this overview of education. A practitioner does not develop expertise in all aspects of graphic design but selects a special area of interest in a particular kind of communication problem. One designer may love print media and therefore prefer magazine or book design. Another may have a great interest in type design or want to design exhibits. Design **education** is a preparation for **practice,** so if a certain kind of design appeals to you, think about what kind of learning supports it. Flip back and forth between this chapter and Chapter 8 as you consider how your education can prepare you for a particular kind of design practice.

Perception, Visual Organization, Aesthetics

Form and Structure

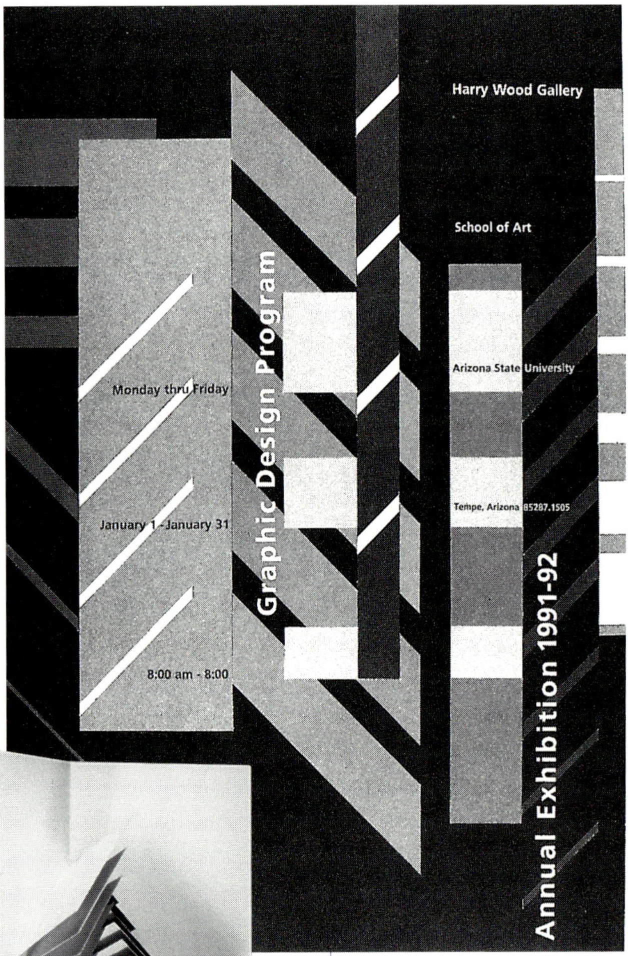

Form Analysis

Graphic designers think about visual forms and how they are put together to convey meaning. These forms are a kind of visual language. Points, lines, planes, volumes, spaces, areas, textures, and colors, as well as how they are used to create symmetry, proportion, and rhythm, are basic aspects of the designer's visual vocabulary.

Form and structure analyzes positive and negative forms.

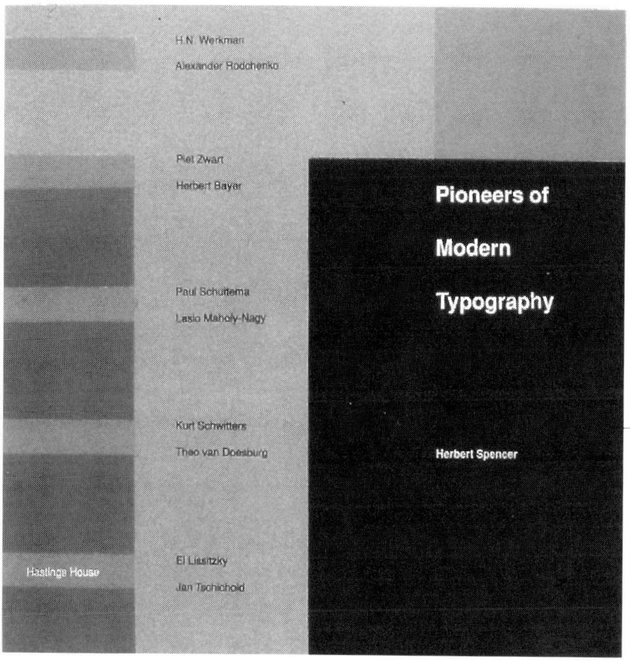

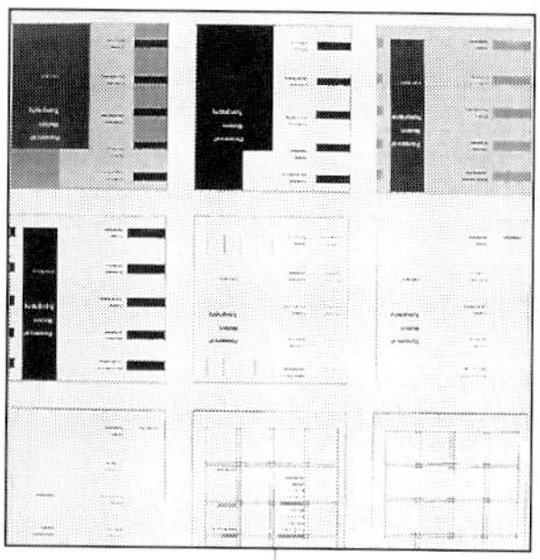

Structure and System

Visual Phenomena

Form analysis examines how two- and three-dimensional forms create a feeling of space.

Structure and system consider various ways to create order in space. For example, a grid system is one way to create a sense of harmony and order.

Visual phenomena explores the intuitive response of the audience to form, color, and texture.

Perception, Visual Organization, Aesthetics

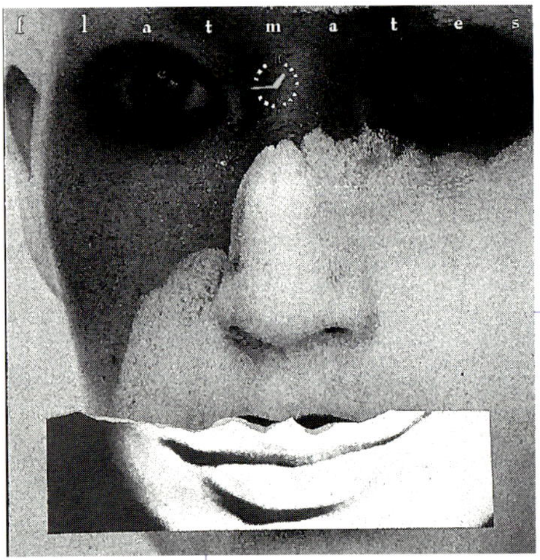

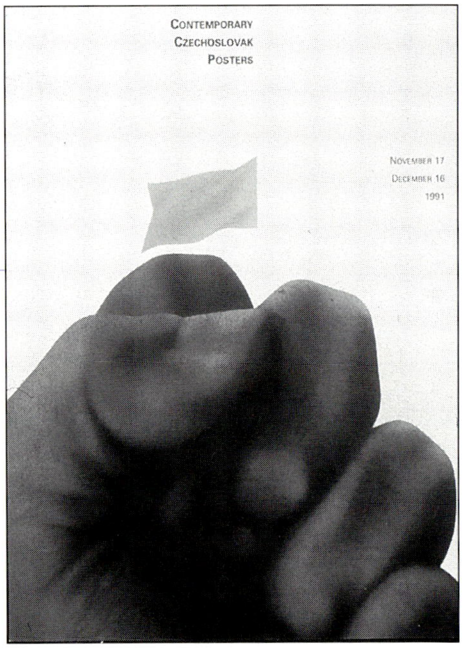

Composition and Visual Framing

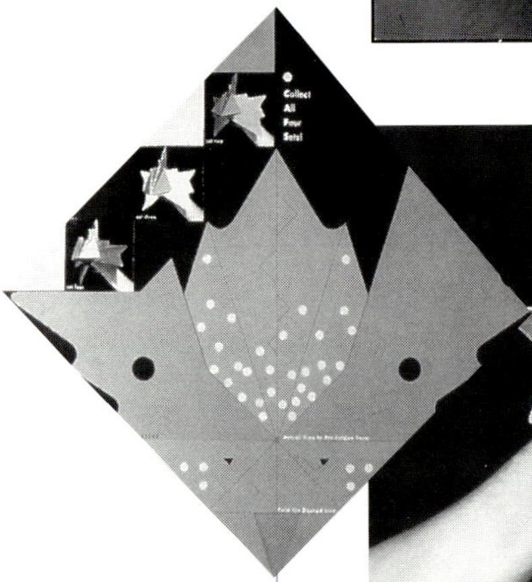

Visual Abstraction

Composition and visual framing involves deciding what to include in an image and how elements of an image contrast with one another.

Visual abstraction identifies the key features of an object and simplifies them.

Unity of form looks at relationships among design elements, such as proportion, scale, symmetry, and contrast.

Visualizing Techniques

Photography

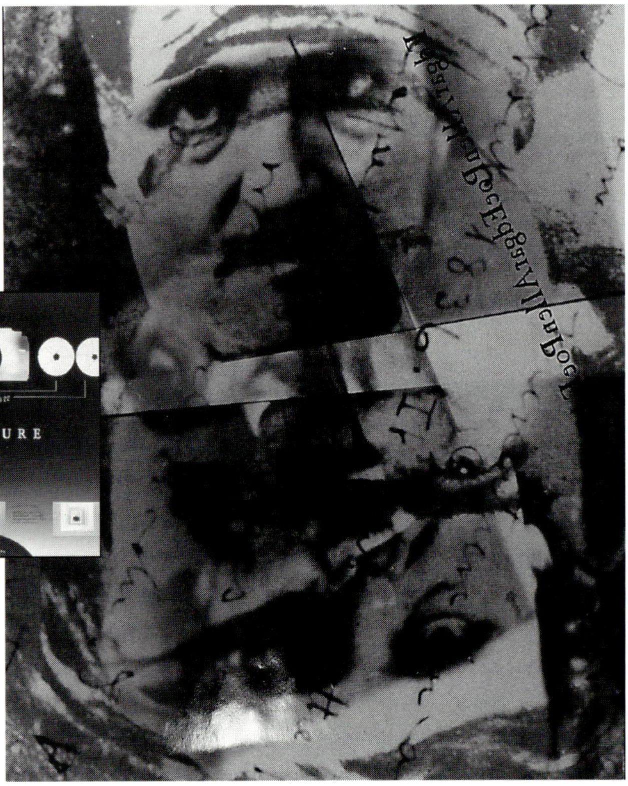

Visual Translation

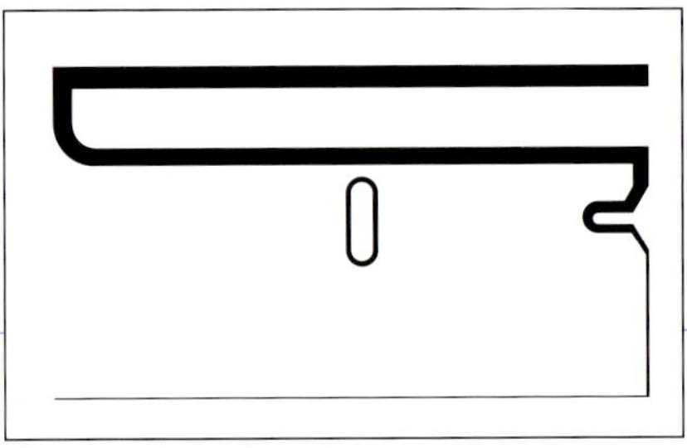

Graphic designers need to be familiar with basic tools, techniques, and processes to produce images, sketches, models, and finished work. They need to use tools with skill and sensitivity. Students learn photography, various kinds of drawing, model making, and diagramming as ways to develop their ideas.

Photography, although often regarded as a "truthful" rendering of the world, may convey realism or emotion, as demonstrated in these examples.

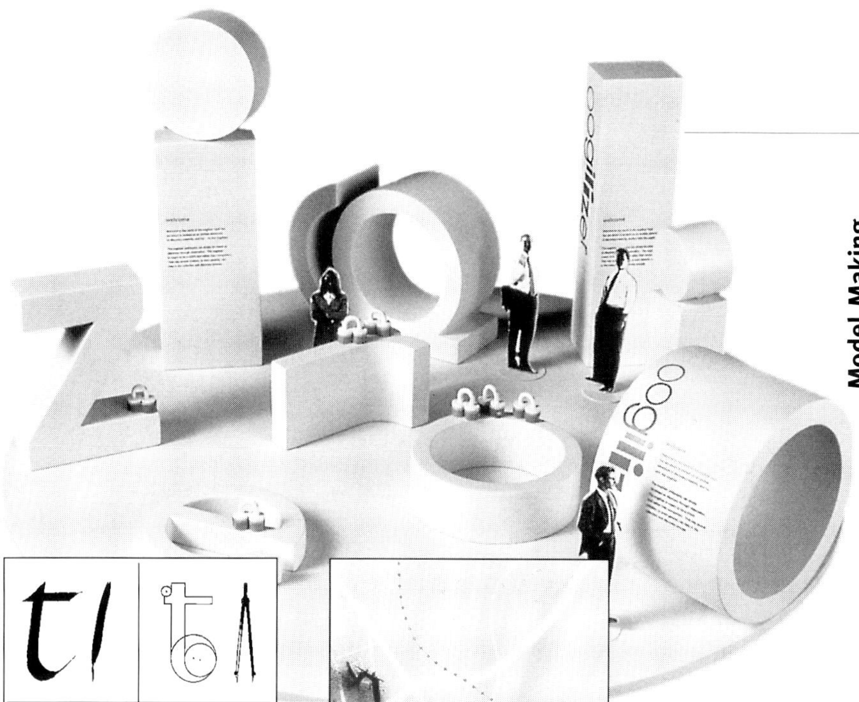

Model Making

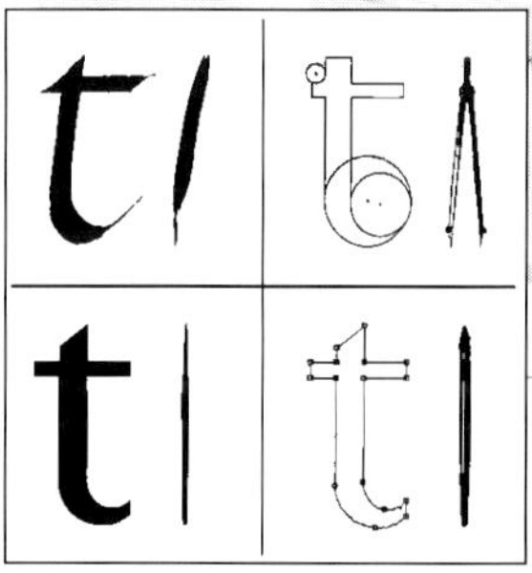

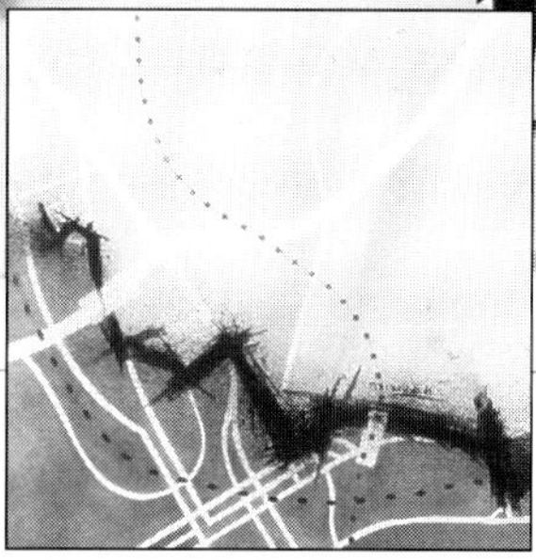

Drawing

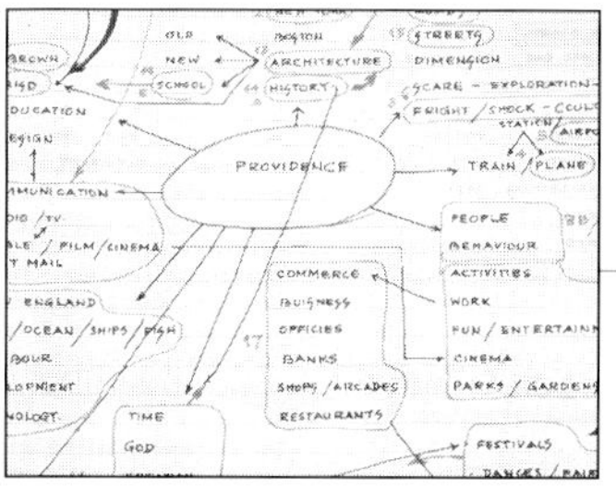

Diagramming

Visual translation is the process by which the essence of an image is abstracted in a drawing.

Model making explores three-dimensional forms in order to plan and prototype an exhibition or a new product.

Drawing teaches the student to look and to see as well as to put down meaningful marks on paper.

Materials, Tools, and Technology

Technology always plays a role in the process of designing and in communicating information visually. Graphic designers create ideas in two and three dimensions using various materials such as paper and film. They use tools such as computers, cameras, and airbrushes and work with the technologies of letterpress and video. The designer's selection of materials and tools can change what an image looks like and what it says.

Blending Ideas and Production Techniques

Graphic designers create solutions to design problems. A part of every solution includes communicating how to get the job done technically: how to get the poster printed or how to create the mechanicals for the package design. The designer must learn to clearly express and transmit ideas and instructions as well as to receive and evaluate feedback. To this end, the student learns to specify technical instructions; to write objectives, briefs, and reports; to present ideas verbally, graphically, and with audiovisual support; and to listen carefully.

Message and Content

Semantics

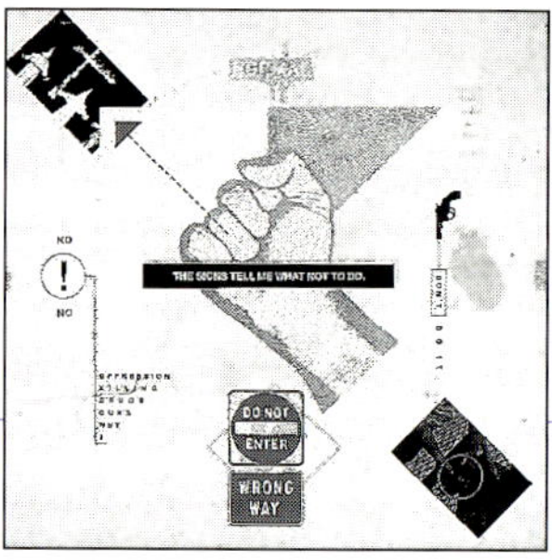

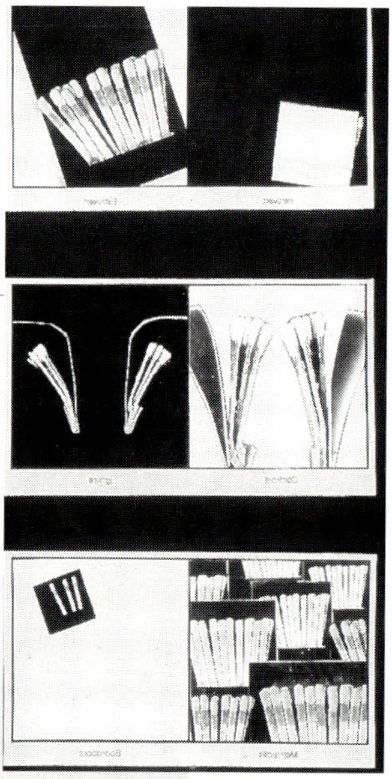

Visual Metaphor

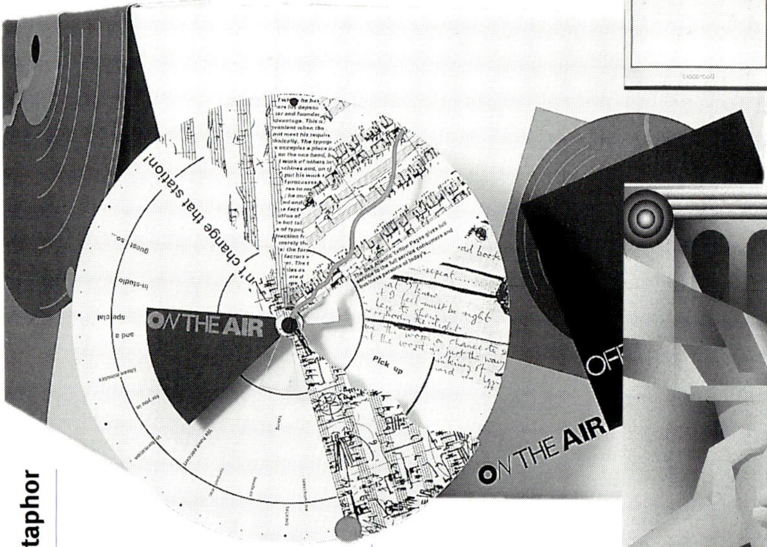

Graphic designers address communication problems. They interpret ideas and represent them with images and words. Skill in thinking about and creating meaning with images, type, and symbols is essential. The ability to put a persuasive or informational perspective on an idea is also important.

Semantics is the study of how people understand words and images.

Persuasion and Information

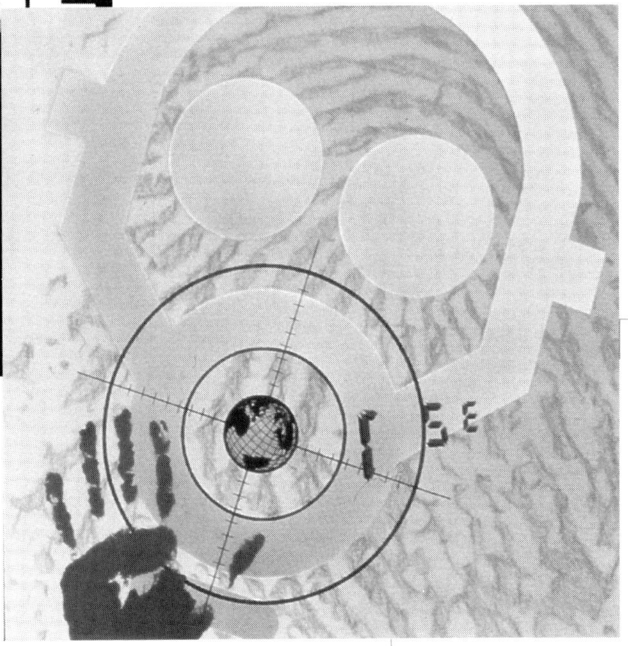

Image, Symbol, and Sign

Visual metaphor studies symbols such as the torch shown here, which can signal the abstract ideas of victory or freedom, for instance.

Persuasion and information examines how to create a memorable visual statement.

Image, symbol, and sign explores the ways in which graphic marks, such as a handprint or a target, communicate.

Methods, Planning, and Management

These Bill of Rights broadsides demonstrate **design planning.** Seminars with legal experts helped the students study the judicial processes of the Supreme Court and specific legal decisions. Students then did additional research and experimented with typography, historical imagery, and the "re-presentation" of photojournalism to determine how to present their ideas visually to a high school audience. The broadsides communicate difficult concepts by identifying specific elements in the Bill of Rights and the landmark Supreme Court decisions that anchor them.

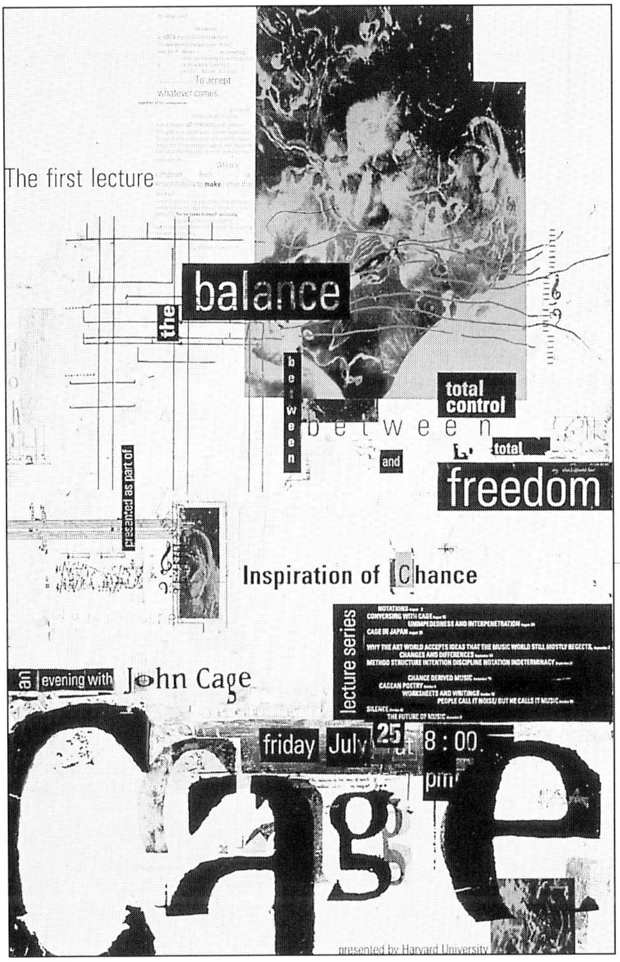

Design Methodology

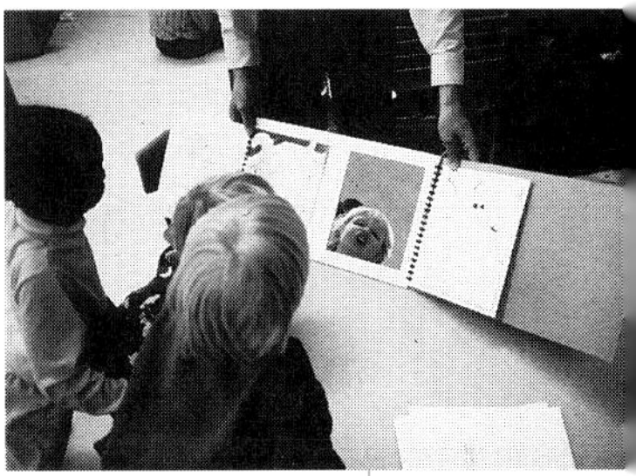

Design Evaluation

Design methodology provides a path for the designer in the search for solutions to communication problems. This path led to an illustration of the creative process in the John Cage poster above.

Design evaluation judges reaction to a design through a testing procedure. For example, observing a child's reaction to a book might answer the questions: Is the book easy to read? Is it appealing? Is meaning communicated effectively?

Design management involves an overview of the process of design, including managing creativity, costs, schedules, and quality. These processes are the invisible components of the designs on this page.

History and Criticism

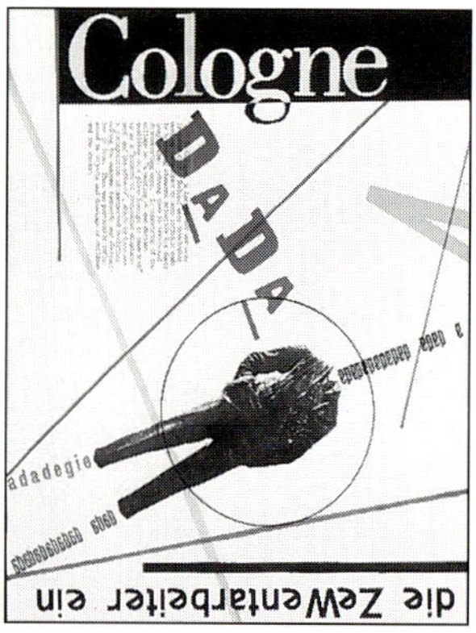

Graphic designers are part of a visual culture that includes art, architecture, and design. It is not only interesting but also important to know what has gone before. Designers study the past for inspiration and to understand its themes, styles, and technical developments. It is possible to trace how certain ideas, developments in the arts, and technological advances have influenced particular designers. The historical examples here show students' understanding of a particular designer or movement. Criticism helps the designer to evaluate the usefulness or beauty of a design.

Design Theory

Design theory explores the principles underlying what communicates and why. For example, why does one color communicate happiness to you and fear to someone from another society? What are the ways culture affects the designer and the audience? Design theory seeks to find the unifying principles—which might be intuitive or deliberate—that are the basis for all graphic design. It is where education and practice meet.

Graphic Design Subjects

Letterform

Typography

Letterform investigations look at the forms of logotypes and letterforms found in everyday objects and in typefaces.

Typography examines text messages created for information or expression.

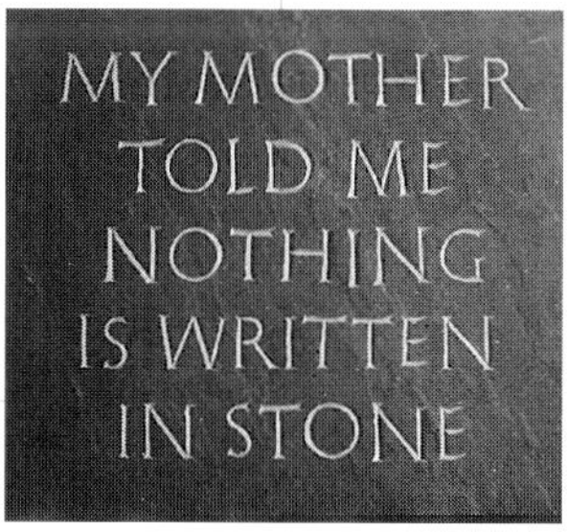

Type and image explores the relationship between the two and the power of each to communicate in relation to the other. Type also becomes image in some applications.

Graphic Design Subjects

Design Systems

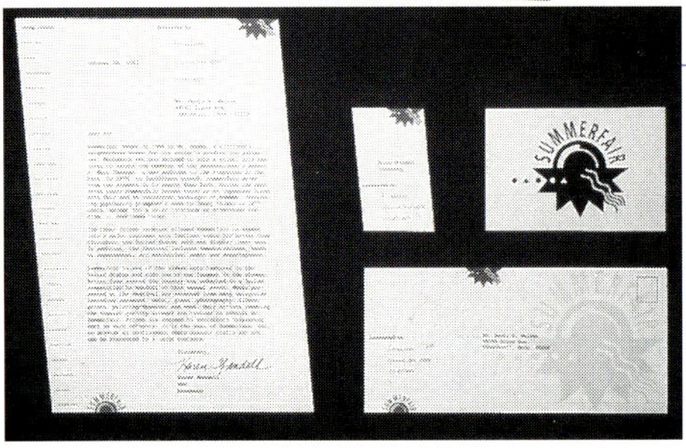

Symbol and Identity Systems

Design systems serve to unify appearance and coordinate production. Visual characteristics, such as the 45-degree angle, the square on its tip, the color, and the torn paper, are played out over many pieces to guarantee an easily recognizable relationship.

Symbol and identity systems seek to specifically identify an object or event for the public and to use that identity in all communications.

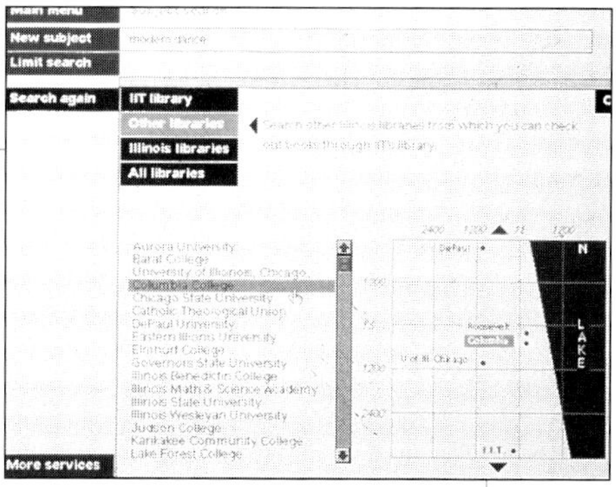

Information Design

Diagrams, Graphs, and Maps

Information design clarifies data, helps orient the viewer, and guides the search for what is important by establishing a clear visual hierarchy. These qualities are particularly useful in computer interface design, as illustrated by the "Need Theories" data base screen and the library-search screen.

Diagrams, graphs, and maps distill information to make it easily understood. "Games of the World" diagrams the playing of a game. The three-dimensional form shows the relationships of solid, liquid, and gas.

Graphic Design Subjects

Publication and Print Design

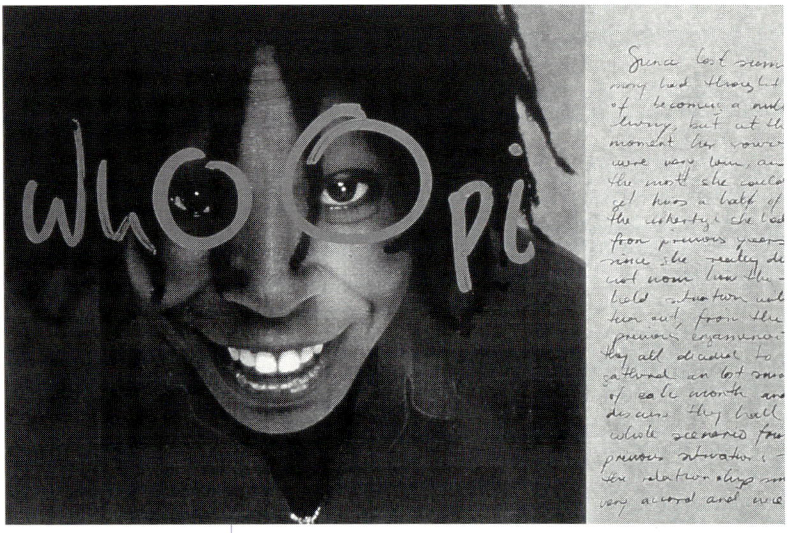

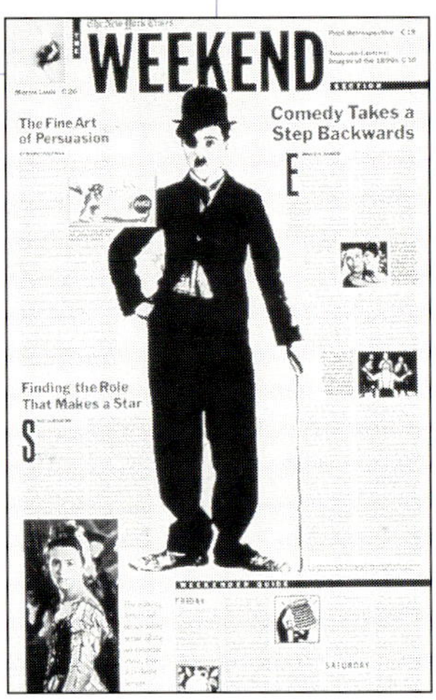

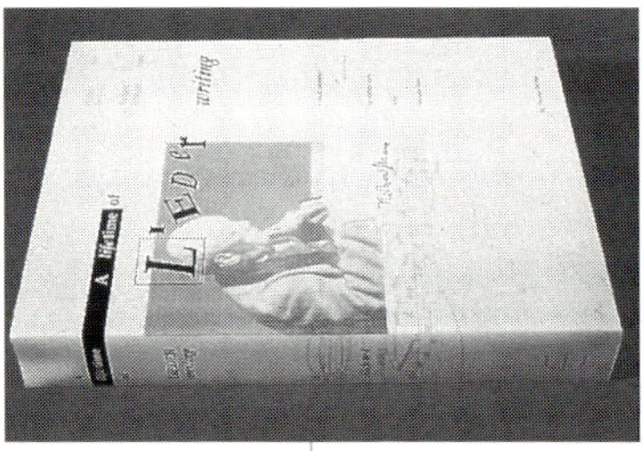

Book Design

Publication and print design explores the overall structure—pacing, sequence, and hierarchy of information—as well as the particular use of text and image found, for example, in the editorial material of magazines and newspapers.

Book design is concerned with both the exterior package of the book (the cover) and its interior contents (the pages).

Poster Design

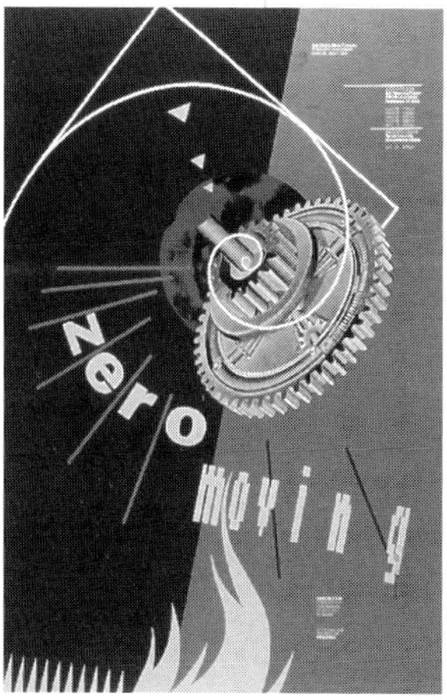

Poster design combines words and images in a powerful public announcement, whether for an art exhibit, an election campaign, or a circus.

Film and video graphics organize ideas dynamically in time. They communicate by using images in sequence with narration, music, and text.

Computer graphics explores the digital world of highly manipulated imagery.

Graphic Design Subjects

Package Design

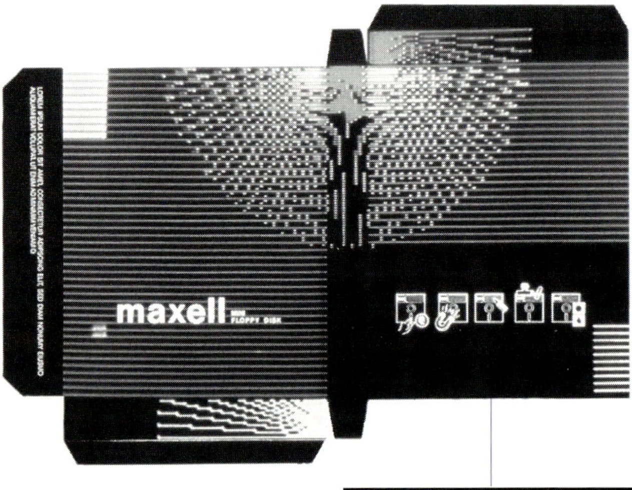

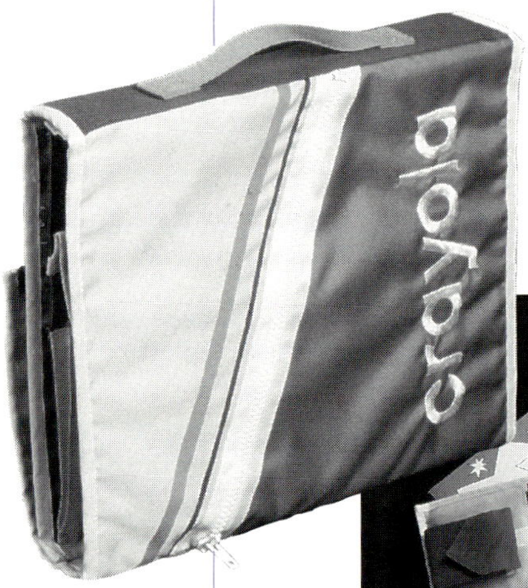

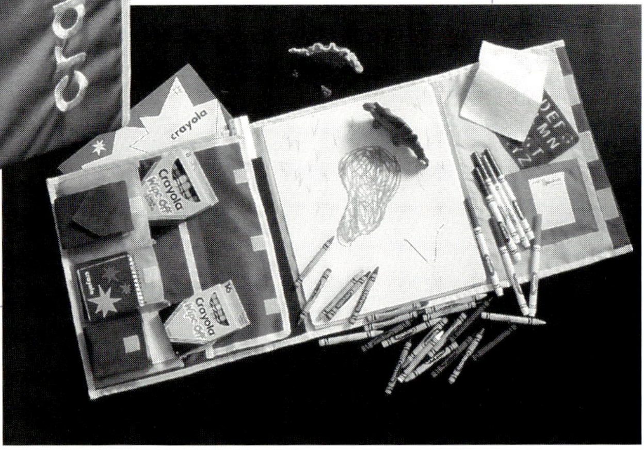

Package design serves multiple functions: to protect, display, dispense, store, and announce the identity and qualities of a product. Bandini and Maxell are traditional packages, and the Crayola package is a concept kit.

Environmental signage and graphics helps people find their way through streets and buildings, and gives clues to the nature of the environment people find themselves in.

Exhibition Design and Display

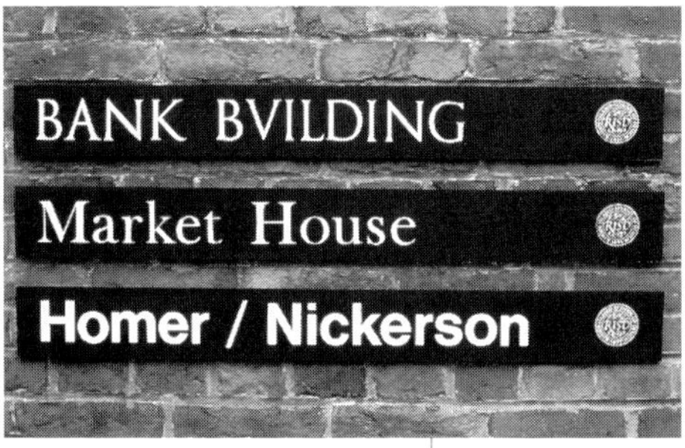

Environmental Signage and Graphics

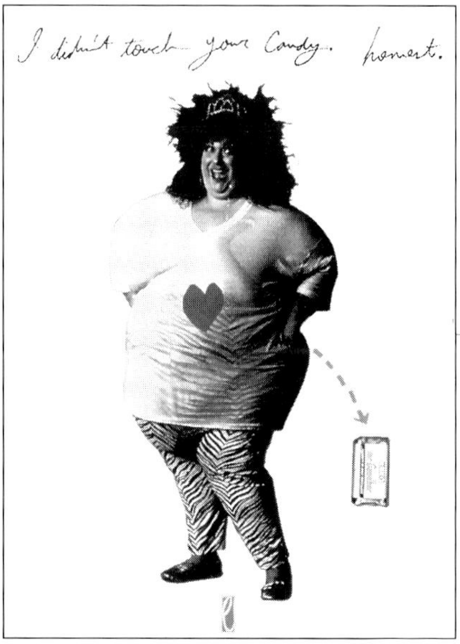

Advertising Design

Exhibition and display design seeks to involve an audience in exploring an idea in space and time through the use of graphics, objects, text, sound effects, and participatory opportunities.

Advertising design is calculated to attract attention, make a compelling pitch to an audience, and create a desire for the product.

Who becomes a graphic designer?

There are probably as many kinds of designers as there are kinds of design, so how do you know whether a career in graphic design might be right for you? First, you might take a look at the clusters of characteristics often shared by graphic designers, and see if you find yourself reflected there. Begin with the three most common traits designers share: interest in the visual world, **curiosity** about communication in all its forms, and creativity.

Designers tend to be skilled "lookers." They take in the world both visually and conceptually. They scrutinize color and texture, they look at relationships between things, and they find the repetition and rhythm in what they see. Conceptually, designers look at an idea from all sides, searching for an approach with a twist—one that goes beyond the ordinary. These habits of eye and mind feed their **creativity.** For designers, the world of objects and ideas becomes an immense playground from which they emerge with fresh ideas and images.

I am an information architect. Architect in my definition doesn't mean style but a kind of rigor in thinking. Information means understanding—and my only passion is to make things that interest me understandable.

Richard Saul Wurman

My early exposure to a design studio made me aware of the design profession as an opportunity to apply analytical abilities to an interest in the fine arts. Graduate design programs made it possible for me to delve more deeply into the aspects of design I found personally interesting. Since then, the nature of the design profession, which constantly draws the designer into a wide range of subjects and problems, has continued to interest me in each new project. It's been this opportunity to satisfy personal interests while earning a living that has made design my long-term career choice.

Won Chung

I like the way words look,

the way ideas can become

things. I like the social,

activist, practical, and

aesthetic aspects of design.

Laurie Haycock Makela

I need to make things that connect in a meaningful, useful, evocative way to others, and I like to indulge in the sensuousness of the material world. I learned that I could use design not only to reach into myself and express my own feelings, but also to reach out to others with images and words that are well researched and thought out, condensed and transformed into a communication that could involve everyday folks in our shared public environment.
Sheila Levrant de Bretteville

As a reflection of their creativity, designers often have an abundance of curiosity. They ask questions, delight in playing the devil's advocate, and are often reluctant to accept someone else's habits or customs. Some say they are "off-center"—more self-directed than they are controlled by society or others. Designers also have intellectual curiosity: they want to understand how communication works, and they are not timid about trying out their ideas on their family and friends. They are interested in the **visual interpretation** of abstract ideas. They draw, they read, they experiment, they make things. They explore culture by participating in it, not only by doing things but also by observing the creative work of others, including attending concerts, seeing films, or just paying attention to life as it goes by. They soak up sensory experience and ideas.

Making things is second nature for designers. Somehow thinking something or saying something just isn't enough. Designers sense intuitively that the process of making something real engages the mind in a different and powerful way: forms and colors change; new ideas

When I was a child, I was obsessed with drawing. At the age of six, when I was confined to a bed for a year as a result of a childhood illness, I found that the only things that kept me busy were building cities out of clay and drawing. Obviously, the urge toward form-making was an important part of my makeup.
Milton Glaser

emerge. They like projects with definite beginnings, middles, and endings because these kinds of projects are tied to development and achievement. Generally, designers dislike routine or maintenance activities. Starting something new and unknown challenges them.

Designers are attracted to things that perform a definite function—things that are **useful** and beautiful. They are interested in improving everyday life rather than creating art for museums. To graphic designers, the limitations of design and communication are seen as challenges rather than as straightjackets.

As you have seen, there really is no exact, ideal, universal designer type. General characteristics—including creativity, openness to new ideas, and a desire to explore the visual world—are more important than specific traits or qualities. Coming from a variety of backgrounds, from all ethnic groups, and from locations as diverse as New York City, Great Plains States, Kansas, and Tokyo, Japan, graphic designers are **different** and seek to refine that difference as they appreciate the differences of others.

I became a graphic designer because my best skill, drawing, did not exercise the rest of my mind.

Colin Forbes

When I was growing up, I wanted to be an artist and an actress. This desire lasted until my second year of college, when I became attracted to design. I took my junior year at design school with the idea of returning to my former college—but I never went back. My destiny was design.

Deborah Sussman

BRODOV
OF ORDER ACHIEVED.
AL
EX
EY
BRODOVITCH

What goes on in design school?

Design education doesn't happen in the typical university lecture hall or laboratory. It takes place in **studios** (literally, places for work) and through **seminars** (organized discussions characterized by informality and high interaction). Learning takes place through the **analysis** of problems and possible solutions using composition, typography, photography, images, and space. Students use materials and processes from basic hand skills to computers to create communications.

Another difference is that design education is **project-based** rather than subject-based. Teachers create projects to reveal certain visual or communication principles or the nature of certain kinds of problems or media. Students learn by doing. From early to late in the curriculum, projects become more complex as students

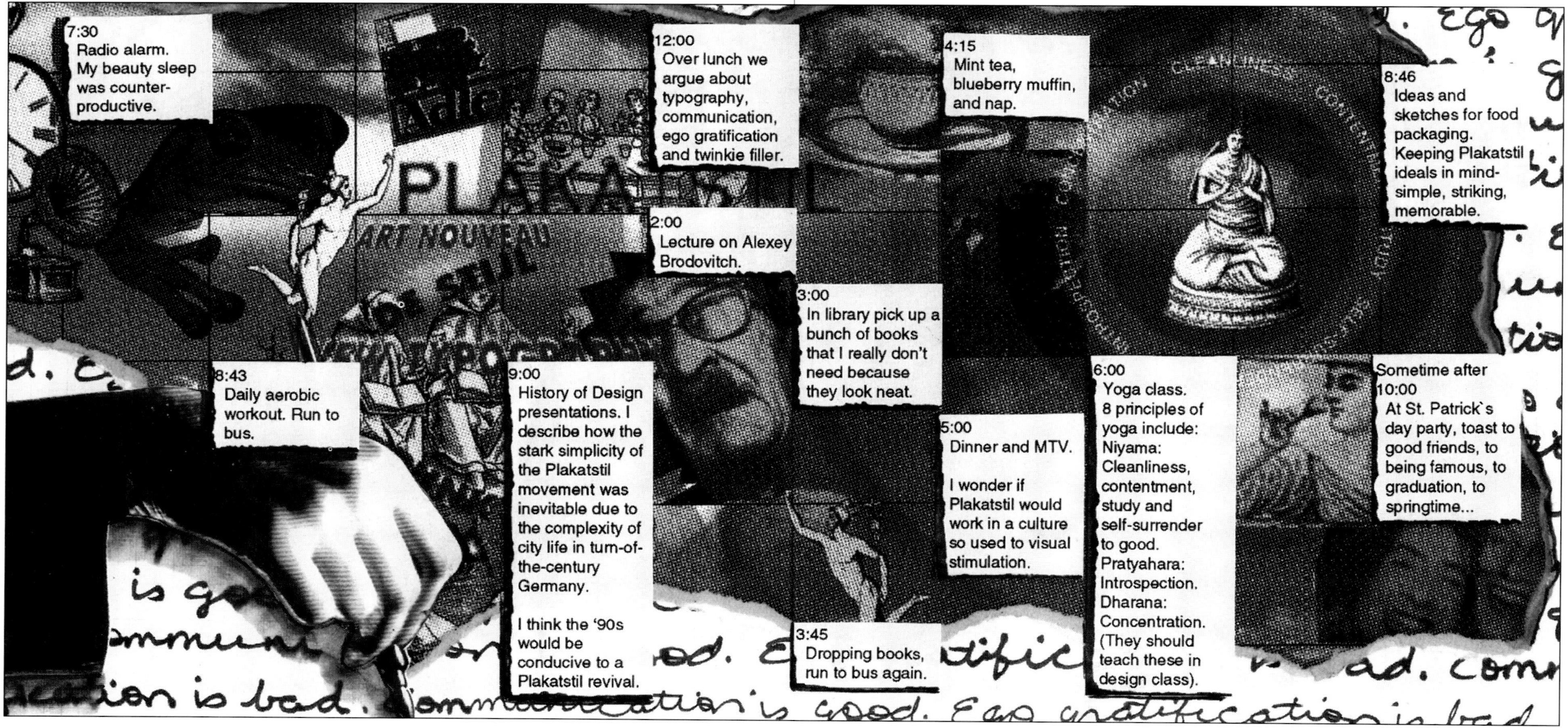
7:30
Radio alarm.
My beauty sleep was counter-productive.
8:43
Daily aerobic workout. Run to bus.
9:00
History of Design presentations. I describe how the stark simplicity of the Plakatstil movement was inevitable due to the complexity of city life in turn-of-the-century Germany.
I think the '90s would be conducive to a Plakatstil revival.
12:00
Over lunch we argue about typography, communication, ego gratification and twinkie filler.
2:00
Lecture on Alexey Brodovitch.
3:00
In library pick up a bunch of books that I really don't need because they look neat.
3:45
Dropping books, run to bus again.
4:15
Mint tea, blueberry muffin, and nap.
5:00
Dinner and MTV.
I wonder if Plakatstil would work in a culture so used to visual stimulation.
6:00
Yoga class.
8 principles of yoga include:
Niyama:
Cleanliness, contentment, study and self-surrender to good.
Pratyahara:
Introspection.
Dharana:
Concentration.
(They should teach these in design class).
8:46
Ideas and sketches for food packaging.
Keeping Plakatstil ideals in mind-simple, striking, memorable.
Sometime after 10:00
At St. Patrick's day party, toast to good friends, to being famous, to graduation, to springtime...
PLAKAT
ART NOUVEAU
ion is bad. communication is good. Ego gratification is bad

build on past experience. From the university's perspective, design education is expensive because it requires that teachers spend time with students individually. No student is anonymous in a design program.

Another aspect of design education is the group **critique.** "Crits" take place at different stages in a project and provide an opportunity to step back and reflect on the project, to exchange critical or supporting ideas, to clarify intentions, and to develop the **ability** to discuss or even defend one's own work—a necessary skill that will later be important with clients. The critique helps students to deal openly with criticism while it trains them in the

7 wake up

8 30 Work on the title design for a friend's character animation film. Titled "**HARLEQUIN**," it's about a disgruntled court jester who attacks his king and subsequently goes insane. I want the title design to foreshadow the jester's evil intentions while staying within the visual context of the drawing. I begin with the typeface *Chevalier* for its Medieval characteristics. Even after "eroding" the letterforms a little, however, they don't convey the feeling I want them to, so I condense the letters and add spikes to reference the castle towers and circle shapes to reference the bells on jesters' caps. I push this approach further to try for a really sinister quality. A big concern now: **Legibility**.

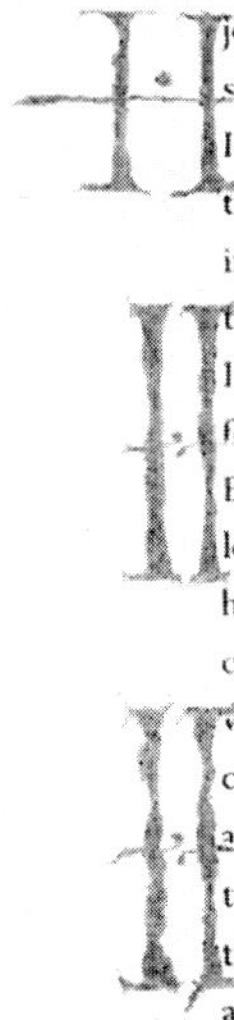

1 4 Design Critique

Individual projects. I'm working on a type exploration of a fictional dialogue between two very different characters: Winnie-the-Pooh (**A.A. Milne**) and Holden Caufield (**J.D. Salinger**). The typefaces and layouts reflect their personalities and their reactions to each other. Type size and letter spacing will show voice inflections. The final format will be a handbound book with a combination of computer printouts and letterpress.

You fell asleep. I hate it when I'm talking and someone just goddam falls asleep right in the middle of what I'm saying and all. I mean it's not *bad* and all but it could give someone a goddam complex or something later on in life maybe. I mean, you gotta kinda feel sorry for kids whose parents never listened to them and later on they have problems and all.

I'm sorry.

I'm only a Little Bear you know.

Classmate's suggestion: for Holden's voice, use Bell Gothic instead of Meta to better represent his internal conflicts.

7 Dance class at a studio in L.A. For **1.5** hours I dismiss all thoughts of design, critical studies, and projects from my mind.

10 Read a few chapters of Stuart Ewen's <u>All Consuming Images</u> for **Design Theory** class.

important **verbal skills** of explaining the reasons behind their solutions. They must go beyond "I like it" or "That stinks." Critiques help students to internalize standards of excellence, to develop a shared vocabulary for discussion, to learn to incorporate useful suggestions from others, and to evaluate their own and others' performances. This process helps students to separate work from self and to acquire the maturity and perspective needed in order to benefit from intelligent criticism. The critique is a basic exercise in **critical thinking.**

Graphic design exists as a response to the need to organize the flow of communication in society. The designer creates the **visual interpretation** of the

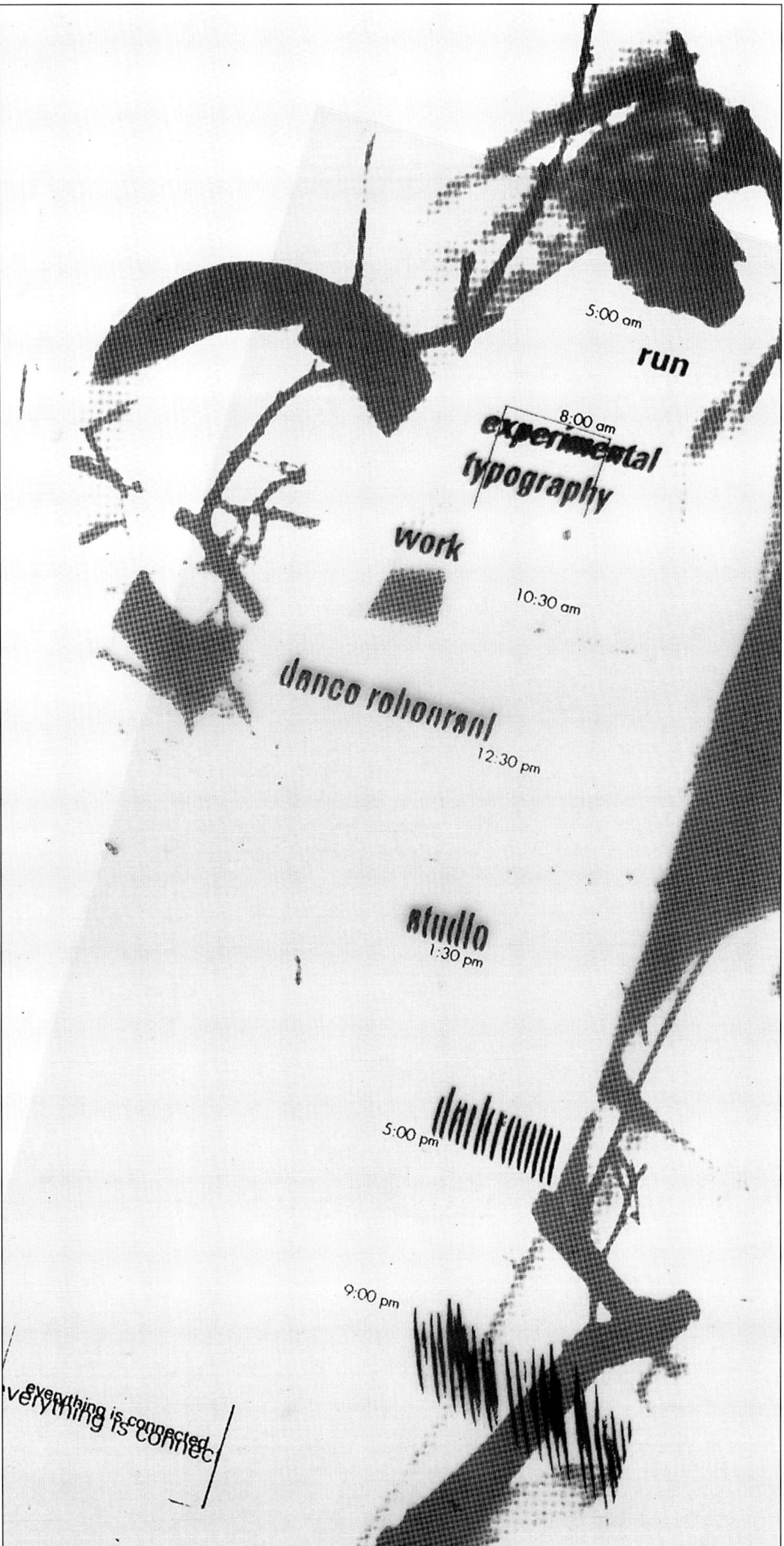
5:00 am
run
8:00 am
experimental
typography
work
10:30 am
dance rehearsal
12:30 pm
studio
1:30 pm
5:00 pm
9:00 pm
everything is connected
verything is connec

message from client to audience. The ways in which the designer chooses to present this information depend on training and on the designer's own personality. That's why design schools spend as much time on the student's path to a satisfactory solution as they do on the solution itself.

Design school students are immersed in **problem-solving** activities. They think spatially as well as verbally; they work in teams and individually; they get things done. As a project-oriented, highly interactive process, design education fosters dialogue, resourcefulness, and a constructive direction for these creative students.

APERTURE

How do graphic design programs differ?

There are hundreds of **graphic design programs** in the United States, and their content and philosophies vary widely. This gives you lots of options, but it also means that identifying the particular programs best suited to your needs and interests can be difficult. The following information can help you understand and compare your **options.**

Graphic design programs are found in a number of different kinds of institutions and in different areas within those institutions. You need to look carefully at each program: its **curriculum,** the ratio of hands-on design work to academic classes in design or other disciplines, and the type of **degree** awarded. You also need to assess your short-term and long-term objectives, the kind of college experience you want, and the kinds of career opportunities available after graduation.

Generally, four kinds of institutions of higher learning can prepare you for a career in graphic design. A **university** will typically offer either a four-year undergraduate program leading to a BS (bachelor of science) or BA (bachelor of arts) degree. Many universities also offer a graduate degree, the MFA (master of fine arts). Within a university, graphic design is likely to be a major in the College of Fine Arts; smaller universities might offer graphic design as a concentration within a fine arts major. Four-year **colleges** offer only undergraduate programs leading to a BA. Typically, graphic design courses are part of the offerings in a fine arts major.

Art schools, often called schools of design or institutes of design, offer a more intensive design education than colleges or universities. On the undergraduate level, four-year programs lead to a BFA (bachelor of fine arts). In an art school, you will usually find a comprehensive graphic design major in its own department. Some art schools also offer the MFA graduate degree.

Two-year programs leading to an AA (associate degree) are available from **community colleges.** These programs are often designed to allow students to transfer credits to a college, university, or art school program. Check requirements carefully to leave your options open.

Because there are exceptions to these typical programs, you should look carefully at the curriculum and degree requirements of any program you are considering. Always make sure that you understand how the program prepares you both for **employment** and for **additional study.**

Particularly important is the number of graphic design courses available versus the quantity of humanities courses (or, in some cases, science courses) available or required. This ratio can be very important to your post-graduate opportunities.

For example, in most college or university programs, students receive a broad **liberal arts education.** Because their design program may not be as comprehensive as art school programs, college students may wish to supplement their education with internships or concentrated summer programs in graphic design, and then get a graduate design degree. However, because designers work with diverse clients whose messages might involve content from abstract art to zoology, a broad exposure to ideas and a well-rounded education are often an advantage. By contrast, art schools offer fewer humanities and social studies courses than colleges or universities, but students are intensively prepared for **current job** opportunities.

An associate degree program in a community college gives students the technical skills to become production artists who prepare art for printing. Graduates might work as assistants in the design or printing industry. These programs give students immediately **marketable skills,** but **advancement** in the field may be difficult without additional study.

How to select a design school

How can you find the design program that's **right for you?** There's no easy answer to this question, but there's bound to be more than one school that will suit your needs. To find them, you will need to ask many questions and to gather facts and impressions concerning curriculum, faculty, facilities, and student body. What you are ultimately searching for is a match between your interests and abilities and the character and opportunities provided by a particular school.

Begin by examining the **subjects** you will be studying—the curriculum. Review the entire curriculum of the graphic design program, course by course, including a short description of each course. What is the **philosophy** of the program? Does the curriculum support it? Do the philosophy and course offerings match your career intentions? What types of courses make up the major emphasis? Do the courses support the description of the major? Does the curriculum allow you a choice of electives? Can you have a minor or a double

Interest in the visual world, drawing skills, an ability to be neat and clear in visual and verbal communication, organization, and an ability to think and solve problems methodically are important to us.

Roger Remington, educator

major if you choose? Who teaches the freshman courses: full-time faculty or graduate students? These freshman courses are among the most important ones you will take because they set the stage for your future development. They should be taught by the most qualified faculty. The curriculum is like a skeleton. In order to function, it should be more than a loose collection of unconnected bones, or unrelated courses.

Depending on the type of school you are looking at, you may need to ask some of the following questions as well: Do the four-year university or college programs have enough breadth and depth in their major (more than a couple of courses)? Do the art schools have a focused major with enough breadth and depth in **studio** courses? Do they have **academics** to support this focus? Do the four-year programs adequately prepare students for graduate study? Are foreign exchange programs available? Are internship programs available, either within

We accept high school graduates purely on the basis of their academic record and potential. Our entering students are among the most academically gifted in the university. We find that intelligent, highly motivated individuals generally excel as design students. Most applicants have not had a sound high school education in the visual arts; consequently we do not evaluate their visual talent.
Gordon Salchow, educator

We look for determination and perseverance, self-confidence as well as talent, in students for our program.

Kevin Byrne, educator

the curriculum or as summer activities? Do the two-year programs have a focused development in marketable design-production specialties? Do they adequately prepare students to transfer to four-year institutions?

While courses, no matter how clearly they are presented, are difficult to evaluate, the credentials of the **faculty** are easier to review. What's more, the composition of the faculty can give you confidence in the curriculum. If the curriculum is the skeleton of a program, the faculty is the heart—these people give life and vitality to the program. Even the best curriculum is little more than a structure representing what can be taught or learned. The faculty makes things happen.

To examine the credentials of the faculty, review the faculty listing found at the back of most college catalogs. It tells where faculty members were educated, how long they have been at this school, their academic rank, what

Students should be critical thinkers, possessing the tenacity to explore and define all facets of a problem. We require more than a formal or stylistic response; we look for innovative problem solvers, able to conceptualize and synthesize information. Also, we expect a professional attitude and work ethic, which are essential to the development of an effective visual communicator. In addition, students must have the interpersonal skills to clearly articulate their ideas and concepts, not only to other design professionals but to a wider audience.

Richard Woollacott, educator

Our mission is to educate socially responsible, visually inventive, intellectually curious, and technologically adept visual communication design professionals. To accomplish this, we must begin with students who excel academically, creatively, and visually. Students who do not first meet our academic profile are not continued in the admissions process. A portfolio provides information about the student's ability to think and communicate visually, but we have less interest in technical draftsmanship than in what ideas capture the student's attention and how these ideas are expressed.

Meredith Davis, educator

courses they teach, and what research or professional areas interest them. Faculties need to refresh themselves, to bring in new members from different places, in order to avoid stagnation. Equally important is faculty activity outside the classroom. Research or professional design activity keeps the faculty members alert and questioning so they can bring new ideas to the classroom.

Also find out the balance between full-time and adjunct or part-time faculty. Full-time faculty provide **continuity** within the curriculum, while adjunct faculty provide specific **expertise** that may not be available from the regular faculty. How many graphic design faculty are there? It is difficult to have a vital curriculum with only one graphic design teacher because there is little **diversity** of ideas, philosophy, or skills for a student to tap into. What is the student-to-faculty ratio in the design program? Design education is highly interactive. Common sense as well as experience indicates

We look for students with strong academic and design viewpoints, with at least a community college background. We look for analytical skills along with design skills. Research, experimentation, and curiosity are also important to us. These are needed to develop good design thinking and to develop form which responds to content!

James Miho, educator

that a high student-to-teacher ratio (more students per teacher) will be a handicap in a design program.

Find out if there is an advising system for the students, one that goes beyond guidance on what courses to take and also provides **counseling** on career opportunities. Is there a placement office on campus and a student advisory board to provide feedback to the school? Are there extracurricular activities such as speaker programs, design exhibitions, and student-run design associations? If possible, tour the school and talk informally with students and faculty. Visit a studio and observe. In brief, try to determine the **quality of life** at the school and within the program.

While you're touring the school, find out about the **facilities,** or physical plant, as well as the atmosphere. Facilities are important; they support the mission of the faculty and the curriculum and contribute to the quality of life. For example, are there enough computer or darkroom facilities to support the instruction? Are they accessible beyond class time so that students can complete projects? Is the equipment maintained? Is there adequate studio space? Is there exhibition space for student work and is it used? Is the **library** well stocked with books and periodicals of interest to design students? Is there a **museum?** A stimulating environment can bring out the best in both students and faculty.

Ask the school to suggest a design alumnus in your area that you can contact. Question the person about his or her experience at the school and about job experience afterward. To find out where other graduates are working, you might ask for a list of alumni and note what kinds of positions they hold relative to how long they have been out of school. Find out which alumni are touted by the school because of their success and why. Ask about **employment potential** in general and for what specific kinds of jobs.

If you have friends or relatives in graphic design or related disciplines, seek them out and ask them about schools and career options. If they cannot answer your questions, maybe they can direct you to someone who can. Look in your local libraries and bookstores for design periodicals (see list in appendix) so that you know what is currently going on in design. Stay in touch with your guidance counselors; information is constantly flowing into their offices, and contact with them keeps them aware of your interests.

Know the importance of the selection process, but don't be intimidated by it. There are many kinds of schools and programs, and there is more than one situation right for you. Some schools are highly selective, but many lesser-known colleges offer a substantial and challenging undergraduate experience. Remember that you are evaluating them just as much as they are evaluating you. Be honest with yourself about your interests and abilities. Then gather both **facts** and subjective **impressions** of school quality and character. Be realistic about the match that's best for you.

I am looking for students who show keen intellectual skills and who are genuinely intrigued with everything that makes up culture (from science and technology to anything that impacts communication, like the social and behavioral sciences, philosophy, and history). I would rather teach visualization skills to a student with a strong intellectual drive who has never drawn an image than work with a student who has only an ability to craft images.
Dietmar Winkler, educator

VICTORY

What do you look for in a recently graduated designer?

How to find your first job

Many young designers find it hard to believe that they can make a living doing something they find compelling and interesting—something they love. Finding the right first job, even if it's a summer job or an internship, is not just an important step in launching your career. It is an exploration of the field and a continuation of the learning process. Even the most skilled designer finds the search for a first job stressful. The suggestions that follow can reduce that stress by providing an **overview** of that process.

Before you can begin your job search, you need to understand **1.** yourself: your motivations, strengths, and weaknesses; **2.** your work: its nature, style, and variety; and **3.** the job market: corporations, design offices, and the wide variety of other businesses that employ graphic designers. Then you can get ready to present yourself and your work in a **portfolio.**

To create a portfolio, select only your **best work**—the work you are proud of and want to discuss. Bearing in

We tend to look for a team worker—someone flexible and nonegotistical—as well as for a great sense of typography, and a good sense of humor. We absolutely need people with skills on the Macintosh computer since 99.9% of what we design and produce is on it.

April Greiman

We take for granted that serious candidates will have strong formal design skills. We look for those who can work at abstract and metaphorical levels and can contribute on a par with writers in developing concepts and themes. In short, we like to find those individuals who define "designer" in the broadest possible terms.

Won Chung

mind that people remember best what is first or last in a sequence, bind together sketches that show your ability to think, to sketch, and to brainstorm. Meanwhile, think about your strengths and weaknesses (we all have weaknesses), and prepare yourself to discuss them in an interview. Because your well-crafted, unique communications can take a beating when they are handled, safeguard your work. Shoot documentary slides of the work for your own record and for a slide portfolio to send to a distant location.

If your school provides courses or advisory sessions for assembling a portfolio and marketing yourself, take advantage of them. Show your portfolio to teachers and attend any portfolio reviews organized by local professional design organizations. Listen to the feedback you get. Identify **special interests** or characteristics that you bring to the work situation as well as what you would like to learn on your first job. You'll want to make

Humor is an attribute I appreciate and look for in anyone with whom I am to share the workplace—not joke-telling but a kind of ironic sparkle. Flexibility is also important—things change, something doesn't turn out the way you thought it would, sometimes errors are made. I look for someone able to accommodate to problems that arise in the process of doing work. Looking at someone's sketches sometimes reveals this openness.
Sheila Levrant de Bretteville

I never look for graphic designers in particular—what I look for is passion. One of the best people I ever hired was an automotive designer. Others in my office didn't want him. For me the question was, How does his mind work? His passion was formidable. (This is not a unique story in my hiring procedure.)
Richard Saul Wurman

clear to your prospective employer that you know learning continues throughout a career. In fact, the learning curve is particularly steep for the first two or three years after you finish school and should continue for the rest of your life.

Everyone looking for a job should have a **résumé,** but this document can be especially important to a design applicant. Your résumé deserves careful typographic design that reflects your type skill and ability. Remember to give the facts an employer wants to know as well as a reliable address and telephone number. It is also a good idea to design and print **stationery** and business cards for yourself. They provide another opportunity to make an individual design statement. Any designer with whom you interview will appreciate the difficulty of designing this material. Designing for yourself is worse than representing a client; it can be like having an identity crisis.

We look for the ability to think and to articulate ideas as well as for basic drawing skills and a feeling for typography and words. The sense that the candidate will function well in a collegial environment is important too.
Tom Geismar

I look for intelligence, persistence, desire, good hands, energy.
Milton Glaser

The next step is to identify the design offices, corporations, or individuals with whom you'd like to interview. School **placement** offices usually have job leads of real value, and they cover the larger organizations that recruit for design positions. Trade magazines and design annuals in your school library are also good resources. If you want to work in a particular geographic location, look for help wanted listings there. Also scan your school's alumni lists for recent graduates in that city. Call them up and discuss your interests with them. **Alumni** know people in design and are often willing to help a recent graduate meet them. Looking for a job is a serious networking activity. This may be the first time you **network,** but it won't be the last.

Prospective employers often prefer to receive a brief letter and résumé before committing to an interview. If possible, use the **letter** to establish your interest relative to a particular job opening or to the organization's specialty. Give the reader of your letter a sense of who you are. Follow

An awareness of contemporary design, passion, typographic instincts, and risk-taking are the essentials for a designer to be hired.

Laurie Haycock Makela

I look for a strong background in traditional typography, including some calligraphic study and metal typesetting experience, in addition to computer-aided typographic design skills. A solid foundation in typography allows the designer to get his or her ideas across more simply and clearly. The ability to take a design from initial concept to final piece is a real plus as well—practical production skills are valuable even in a first job.

Carol Twombly

What do you look for in a recently graduated designer?

I presume design competence (it isn't that hard to achieve); then I look for interest in the world outside design. If designers are curious, then I'm interested. If not, my interest evaporates, because design itself is about nothing, it's only a language and languages are used to communicate different kinds of messages and ideas.
Tibor Kalman

up with a telephone call to arrange an appointment. The person you are contacting is probably a busy professional, so don't be easily discouraged. Be politely persistent if you do not get an appointment immediately. Sometimes you will get an interview with someone who has no job openings but is still willing to meet with you. Take this "exploratory" interview. It will be excellent practice, and you may be more relaxed if your dream job is not on the line. What's more, this individual may help you make other connections.

The first **interview** is always the most stressful, so arrange mock interviews with friends to get practice and feedback. At the real interview, try to relax. Remember to breathe. If you don't see design work displayed, ask to see some. Ask questions about the organization and its projects. Be interested in them; then explain how you can help with their needs. Don't drone on about yourself; be attuned to the interviewer's verbal responses and body language. An interview, when it really works, is a dialogue

Generally we look for technologically sophisticated designers. Of course I would like them to be physically adept at making things too. They need to be able to develop concepts and have good interpersonal abilities. We need team players, not loners.
Deborah Sussman

Applicants must demonstrate a sensitivity to typography in their résumés. Their portfolios should be carefully crafted with inventive work. Applicants must be intelligent and articulate. Their references should describe them as collaborative team players.

Anne Ghory-Goodman

between people who are sharing information and finding common ground. After any interview, always stop to record your impressions. A follow-up note of thanks will be appreciated as a courtesy and is a way to help interviewers remember you.

When you are offered a job, you may be taken by surprise and neglect to negotiate. Don't just blurt out a "yes." Employers will respect your taking time to consider the conditions of employment. This is your opportunity to establish your **market value** as a designer. Figure out what it takes to live reasonably in the city under consideration, and don't forget your educational loans. Try to find out what entry-level design salaries are in that area, and balance that information against your personal strength as a designer. Remember, in addition to money, other things are negotiable, such as health benefits, paid vacations, unpaid leave days, starting date, flexible hours, or months to a performance review (and hopefully a raise). You can sacrifice some of these items for others that are more important to you. Be clear about the offer, ask questions, and take time to **consider** it. Try to adjust whatever is not satisfactory now. It is important to start off a relationship with clarity and trust. After you accept the position, celebrate—but don't throw out your contacts. Send them a note announcing your new position.

Finding your first design **job** means matching your creativity and skill with an organization's real needs. It is also a valuable learning experience. While you are looking, you are learning about the various ways design is practiced. Your next job search—whether it occurs soon or well down the road—will be easier; you will have gained a clearer vision of the field and how you want to position yourself within it. Remember to communicate, to follow up, and to be courteous. That way, you'll take away from this first stressful experience some valuable information, increased confidence, and **satisfaction.**

We respond to graphic skills and intelligence.
Colin Forbes

We want students to understand their responsibility associated with design as a means of educational, social, and public communication. To that end, their ability to interpret, analyze, question, and connect seemingly disparate elements is critical. They need to be visually innovative and curious, to be more concerned with message than style, to aspire to a seriousness of purpose, and to recognize the potential to contribute to the larger goals of society and business. They need to think abstractly, ultimately to be creative and committed, to be educated rather than trained, to be responsive to needs, and to identify opportunity.
Doug Wadden

ROBBIE 68 ROBERTSON THE ROLLING
STONE 68 INTERVIEW BY ROBERT PALMER
STONE 68 INTERVIEW BY ROBERT PALMER

Graphic designers at work

What do professional graphic designers really do? This question needs to be asked in order to answer why you need a design education and what you need to study. The projects created by graphic designers give form to the communication between their client and an audience. To do this, designers ask: What is the nature of the client? What is the nature of the audience? How does the client want to be perceived by the audience? Graphic designers also explore the content of the message the client wishes to send, and they determine the appropriate form and media to convey that message. They manage the communication process, from understanding the **problem** to finding the **solution.** In other words, graphic designers develop and implement overall **communication strategies** for their clients.

Some of the **projects** presented in this chapter will probably seem familiar because of their broad exposure in the media. Others, which are limited to a particular audience, may surprise you. Here you'll see that graphic design arrests attention, identifies, persuades, sells, educates, and gives visual delight. There is a streak of pragmatism in American culture—our society tends to focus on results. The following pages are full of **excellent results**—results that demonstrate the range of activities called graphic design.

The processes that went into creating these design projects are often invisible, but the designer's own words describe the significant **strategies.** In a few cases, you will even see early sketches for a design. It's clear that some projects, because of their size, would be inconceivable without considerable project **management** skills. And the range of content clearly demonstrates the graphic designer's need for a good liberal arts education to aid in understanding and communicating diverse design **content.**

The projects that follow represent various **media,** such as print (graphic design's historic medium) and three-dimensional graphic design media, including environmental design, exhibitions, and signage. Electronic media, such as television and computers, as well as film and video are also represented. Various kinds of **communication** are included, from corporate communications to publishing and government communications. Some projects focus on a specialization within graphic design, such as corporate identity programs or type design. Information design and interface design (the design of computer screens for interactivity) reflect the contemporary need to streamline information and to use new media effectively.

In addition to the projects covered in this chapter, three designer **roles** are also highlighted. Developed over a lifetime, these careers go beyond the commonly understood role of the graphic designer. The corporate executive oversees design for a large company; the university professor teaches the next generation of designers and thus influences the future of the field; the design entrepreneur engages in design initiation as an independent business. Consider these and other design-related roles as you plan your studies and early job experience.

The projects and designers in this chapter were selected to illustrate the range of graphic design activities and to represent the **exceptional** rather than the ordinary. Seeing the best can give you a glimpse into the possibilities that await you in the competitive, creative, and rewarding field of graphic design.

Digital Design

Digital design is the creation of highly manipulated images on the **computer.** These images then make their final appearance in print. Although computers have been around since the forties, they were not reasonable tools for graphic designers until the first Macintoshes came out in 1984. April Greiman was an early computer enthusiast who believes that graphic design has always been involved with technology. After all, Gutenberg's fifteenth-century invention of movable type created a design as well as an information revolution.

Greiman's first interest was video, which led naturally to the computer and its possibilities. She bought her first Mac as a toy, but soon found it an indispensable **creative tool.** "I work intuitively and play with technology," says Greiman. "I like getting **immediate feedback** from the computer screen, and I like to explore alternative color and form quickly on-screen. Artwork that exists as binary signals seems mysterious to me. It is an exhilarating medium!" She wants to design everything and to control and play with all kinds of **sensory experience.**

I didn't have the math skills (so I thought) to become an architect. My high school training in the arts was in the "commercial art" realm. Later at an art school interview I was told I was strong in graphic design. So as not to humiliate myself, not knowing what graphic design was, I just proceeded onwards . . . the "relaxed forward-bent" approach, my trademark!
April Greiman

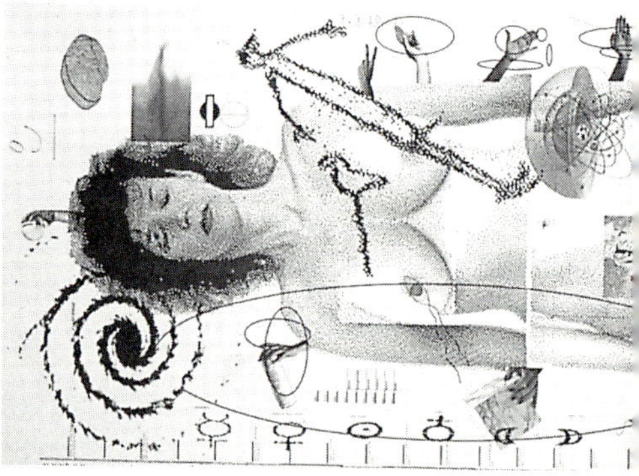

All the work shown on these pages was created on the computer. Then the printer translated it from digital information into its final form—magazine, billboard, or book cover. The *DQ Magazine* art represents the first time Greiman used a Macintosh as a real professional tool: she sent a stack of 8½ x 11 paper right off the computer printer as final art. The Walker billboard concept emphasizes graphic-design techniques: each of the four strips reflects the **technology** on which it was based—steel engraving, offset printing, video, and digital computer. These graphics went from screen to eighty-foot billboard with digital ease. The *AIGA Annual* book cover (page 76, top left) portrays the four elements: fire, air, earth, and water. Computer manipulation allowed the images to converge, making a single, **dynamic image.**

Designers working with digital design need to be more than technicians. Consequently, their studies focus on perception, aesthetics, and visual form-making as well as on technology.

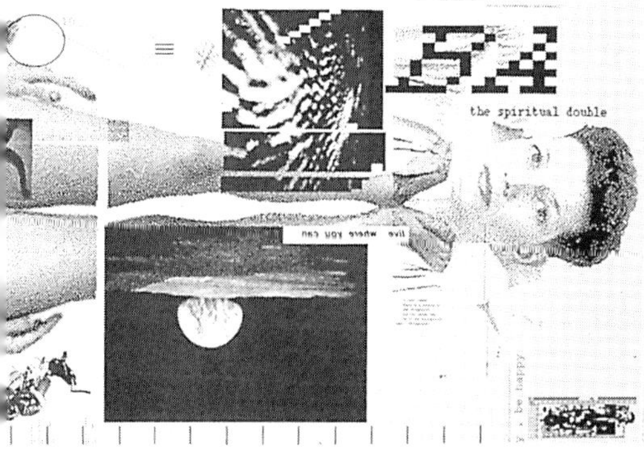

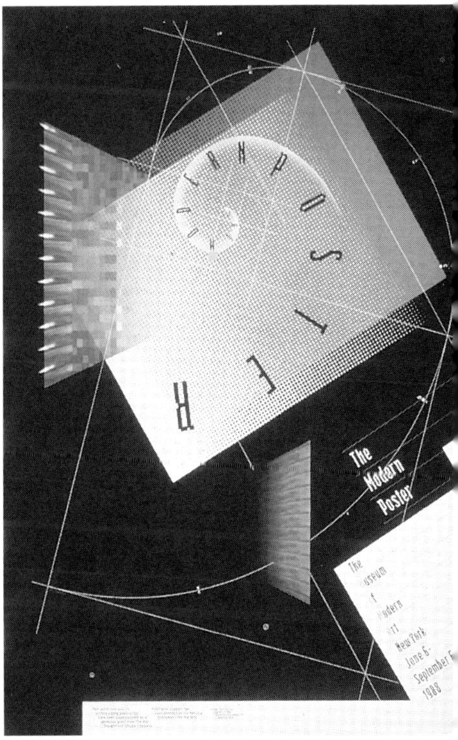

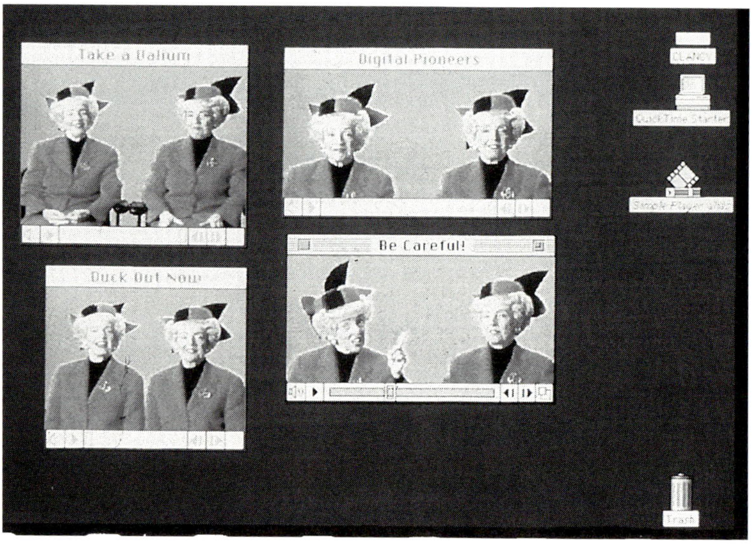

Multimedia Design

The book remains our primary way of delivering information. Its form has not changed for centuries, and its internal organization—table of contents, chapters, glossaries, and so forth—is so commonplace that we take it for granted. But now a challenger has appeared: the **computer.** No longer merely a tool for preparing art for the printer, the computer is an information **medium** in itself.

Computer-based design delivers information according to the user's particular interest. Information is restructured into webs that allow entry from different points, a system that may be more like our actual thinking processes than the neat order of the book is. On the computer, the designer can use time and sound in addition to text and image to draw attention, to animate an explanation, or to present an alternative way to understand a concept. This new technology demands designers who can combine **analysis** with **intuition.**

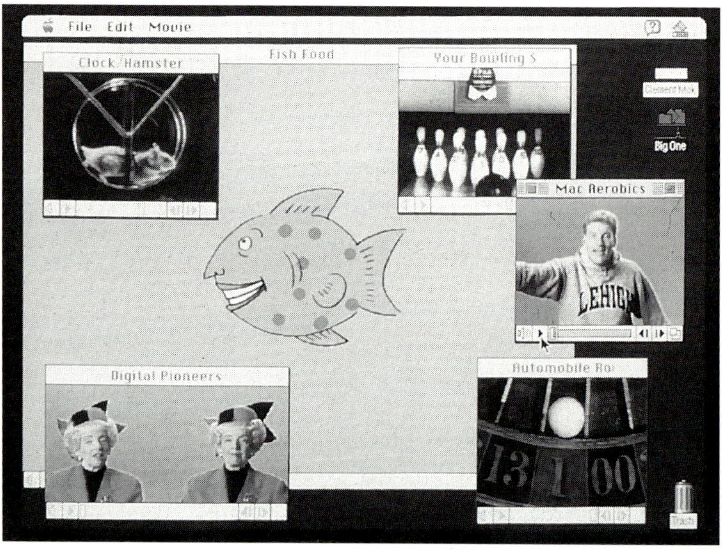

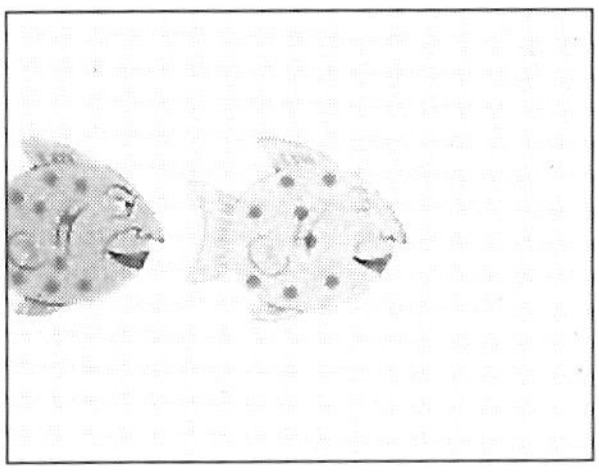

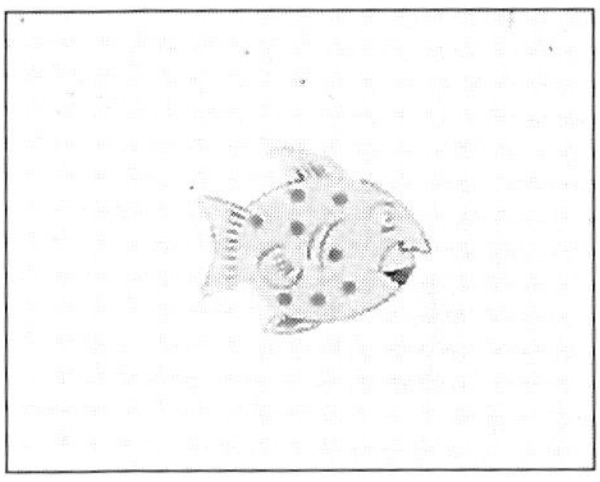

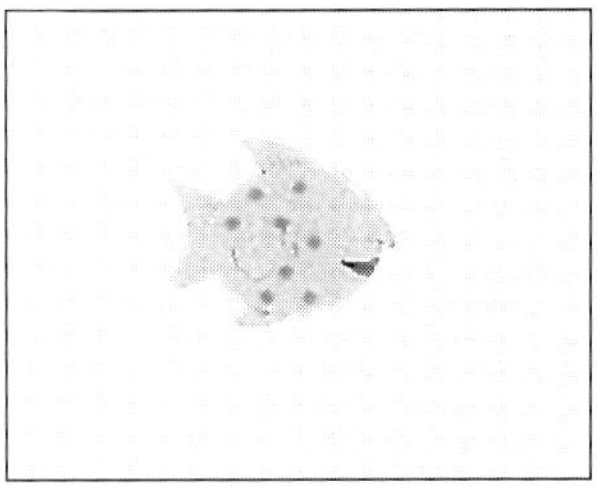

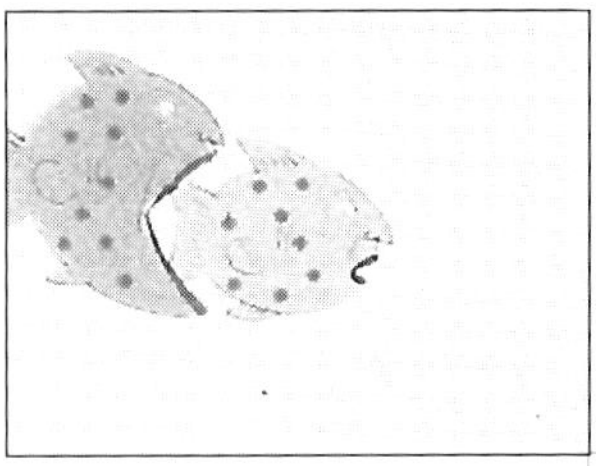

Clement Mok does just that. He is a certified Apple software developer (he can program) and a graphic designer comfortable in most media. QuickTime system software, recently released by Apple, supports the capability to do **digital movies** on the Macintosh. As system software, it is really invisible. "Providing users with this great technology isn't enough," says Mok. "You also have to give them ideas for what they can do and samples they can use."

Mok addressed this problem by developing **QuickClips,** a CD library of three hundred film clips ranging from excerpts of classic films to original videos and animations created by his staff. These fifteen- to ninety-second movies can be incorporated into user-created presentations. It is like having a small video store in your computer. The QuickClips shown here reveal a wry sense of **humor** and do not take themselves too seriously. With them, Mok opens new avenues for presentation with the computer.

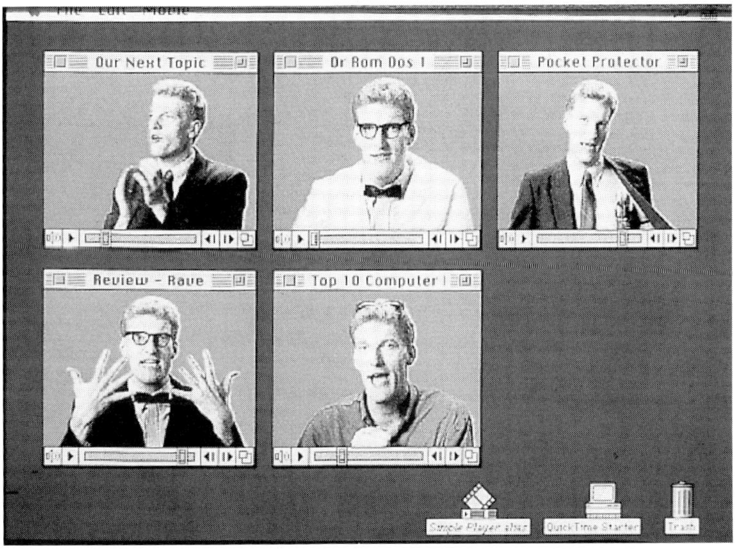

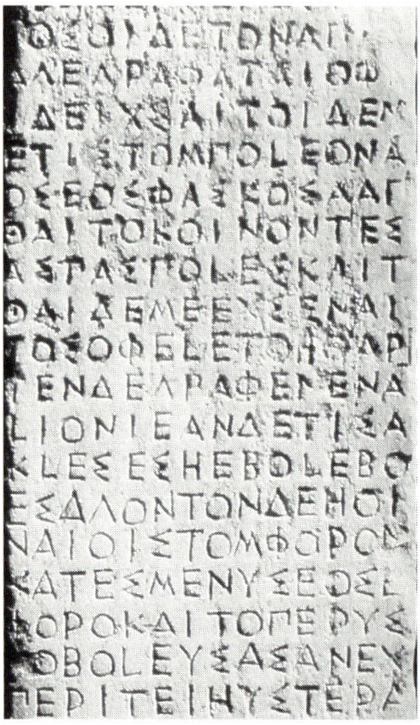

Type Design

It is easy to overlook type design because it is everywhere. Typically we read for content and ignore the familiar structural forms of our alphabet and its formal construction in a typeface. Only when the characters are very large, or are presented to us in an unusual way, do we pay attention to the beautiful **curves** and **rhythms** of repetition that form our visible language.

Since Gutenberg's invention of movable type in the mid-fifteenth century, the word has become increasingly technological in its appearance. Early type was cast in metal, but today's new type design is often created digitally on the computer through a combination of **visual** and **mathematical** manipulation.

The history of culture can be told through the history of the letterform. The lineage of many typefaces can be traced back to Greek inscriptions, medieval scribal handwriting, or early movable type. **Lithos,** which

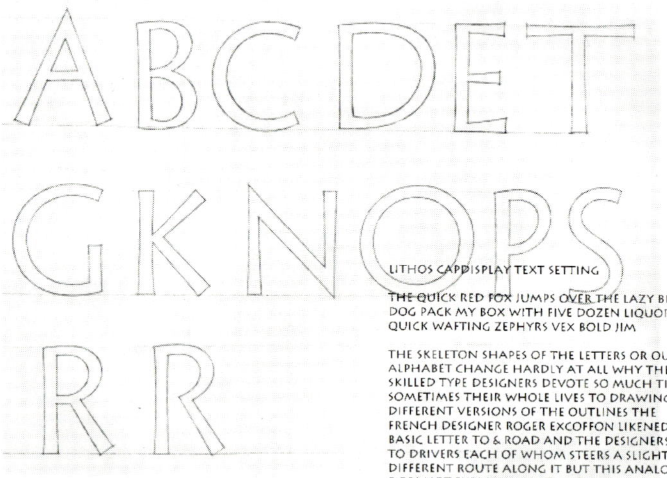

LITHOS CAPDISPLAY TEXT SETTING

THE QUICK RED FOX JUMPS OVER THE LAZY BROWN DOG PACK MY BOX WITH FIVE DOZEN LIQUOR JUGS QUICK WAFTING ZEPHYRS VEX BOLD JIM

THE SKELETON SHAPES OF THE LETTERS OR OUR ALPHABET CHANGE HARDLY AT ALL WHY THEN DO SKILLED TYPE DESIGNERS DEVOTE SO MUCH TIME SOMETIMES THEIR WHOLE LIVES TO DRAWING DIFFERENT VERSIONS OF THE OUTLINES THE FRENCH DESIGNER ROGER EXCOFFON LIKENED THE BASIC LETTER TO & ROAD AND THE DESIGNERS TO DRIVERS EACH OF WHOM STEERS A SLIGHTLY DIFFERENT ROUTE ALONG IT BUT THIS ANALOGY DOES NOT EXPLAIN WHY THESE DRIVER GOT INTO THEIR CARS IN THE FIRST PLACE RUDOLF KOCH THE GERMAN CALLIGRAPHER AND TYPE DESIGNER WROTE THE MAKING OF LETTERS IN EVERY FORM IS FOR ME THE PUREST AND THE GREATEST PLEASU AND AT MANY STAGES OF MY LIFE IT WAS TO ME WHAT A SONG IS TO THE SINGER A PICTURE TO THE PAINTER A SHOUT TO THE ELATED OR A SIGH TO THE OPPRESSED IT WAS AND IS FOR ME THE MOST HAPPY AND PERFECT EXPRESION OF LIFE BY NO MEANS ALL THE DESIGNERS MENTIONED IN THIS BOOK OPERATED AT THIS LEVEL OF CREATIVE ECSTASY BUT ALL WERE DRIVEN BY A LOVE OF LETTERS AND A BURNING DESIRE TO ADD REFINEMENTS TO THE COMMON STOCK OF PRINT

Type Design
Adobe Systems, Inc., Typographic Department
Established 1986
Mountain View, California

means "stone" in Greek, was designed by Carol Twombly as a **classically inspired** typeface. She examined Greek inscriptions, such as the one shown here from 447 B.C., before attempting to capture the spirit of these letterforms in a type system for contemporary use.

Lithos was not an exact copy from history nor was it created automatically on the computer. Hand **sketches,** letterform development on the computer, and trial settings that used the typeface in words and sentences were developed and evaluated. Some were judged to be too stiff, some "too funky," but finally one was just right. These were the early steps in the search for the form and **spirit** of the typeface. Later steps included controlling the space between letters and designing the variations in weight for a bold font. Twombly even designed foreign-language variations.

Clearly, patience and a well-developed **eye for form** and system are necessities for a type designer.

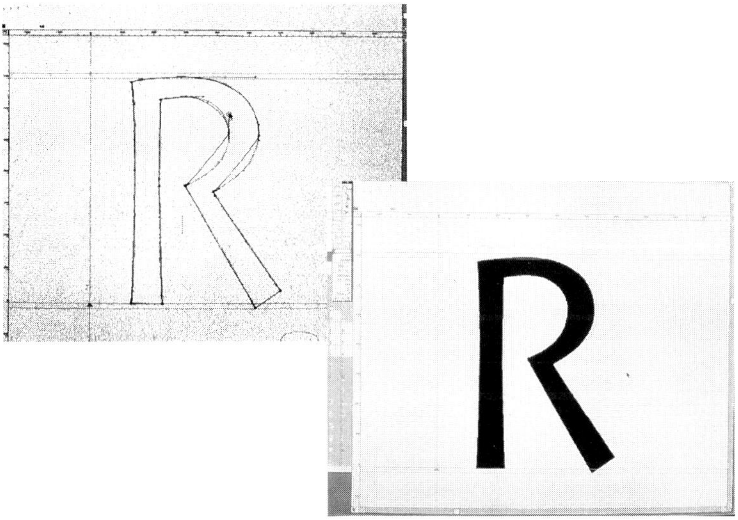

As a kid, when I wasn't climbing trees, skiing, or riding horses, I was drawing and sculpting simple things. I wanted a career involving art of some kind. The restrictions of two-dimensional communication appealed to my need for structure and my desire to have my work speak for me. The challenge of communicating an idea or feeling within the further confines of the Latin alphabet led me from graphic design into type design.
Carol Twombly

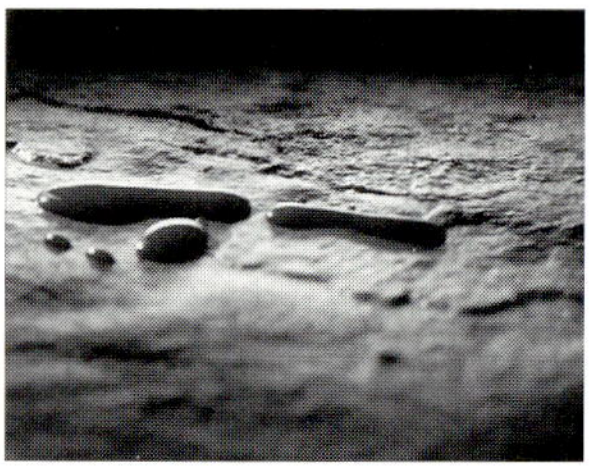

Film Title Design

Most people have had the experience of losing themselves in a film but probably haven't given much thought to the transition we go through mentally and emotionally as we move from reality to fantasy. Film titles help to create this transition. The attention narrows, the "self" slips away, and the film washes over the senses. Film titles set the **dramatic stage;** they tune our emotions to the proper pitch so that we enter into the humor, mystery, or pathos of a film with hardly a blink.

Rich Greenberg is a traditionally schooled graphic designer who now works entirely in film. His recent *Dracula* titles are a classic **teaser.** He begins with the question: What is this film about? Vampires. What **signals** vampires for most of us? Blood. Greenberg believes that a direct approach using the simplest idea is usually the best. "What I do in film is the opposite of what is done with the print image. *Dracula* is a very good example of the process. There is very little information on the screen at any time, and you let the effect **unfold** slowly so the audience doesn't know what they're looking at until the

Film Title Design
RGreenberg and Associates
Established 1977
New York City and Los Angeles

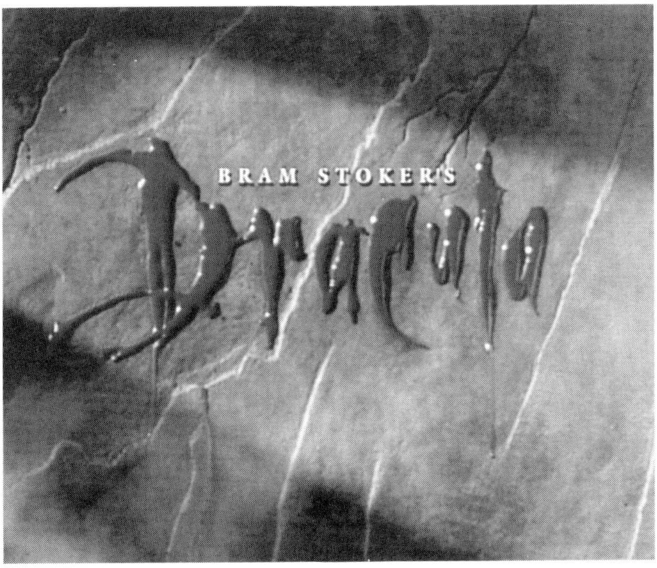

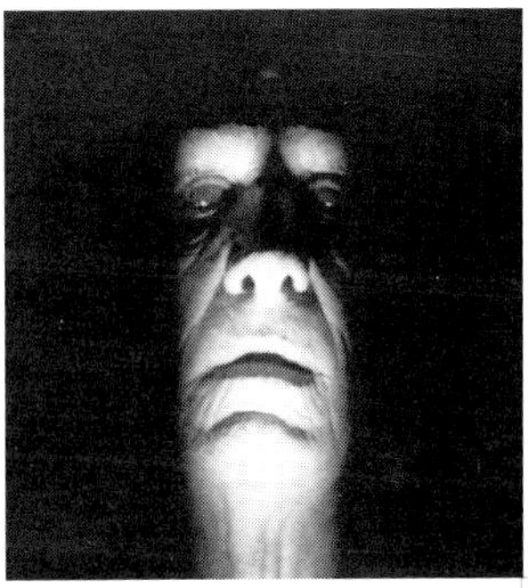

very end. In print, everything has to be up front because you have so little time to get attention. In film, you hold back; otherwise it would be boring. The audience is captive at a film—I can play with their minds."

Special effects are also of interest to Greenberg. In *Predator,* the designer asked, How can I create a feeling of fear? He began by exploring the particular possibilities for horror that depend on a monster's ability to camouflage himself so he seems to disappear into the environment. The designer's **visual problem** was to find a way for the object to be there and not be there. It was like looking into the repeating, diminishing image in a barber's mirror. To complicate matters, the effect needed to work just as well when the monster was **in motion.**

Whether designing opening titles or special effects that will appear throughout a film, designers have to keep their purpose in mind. According to Greenberg, "Nobody goes to a film for the effects; they go for the **story.** Effects must support the narrative."

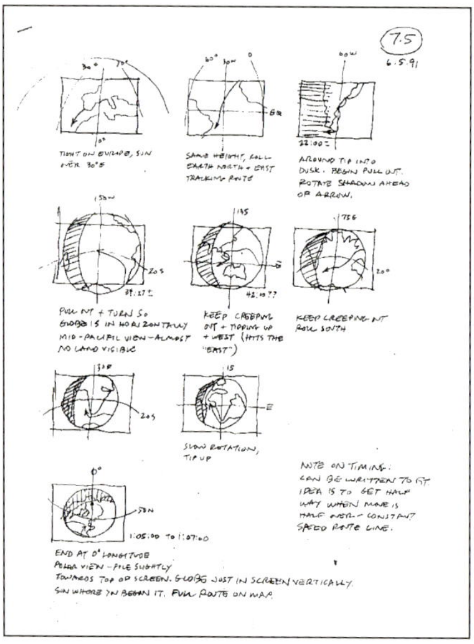

Television Graphics

Motion graphics, such as program openings or graphic demonstrations within a television program, require the designer to choreograph space and time. Images, narration, movement, sound and music are woven into a **multisensory** communication.

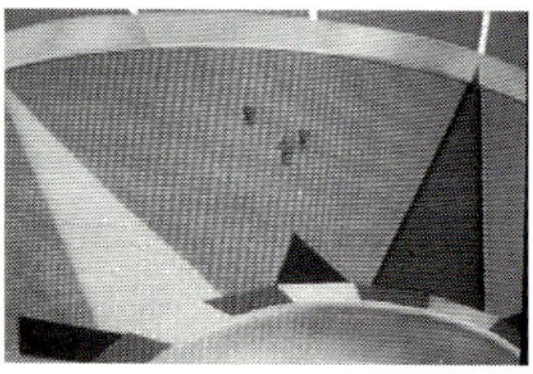

Chris Pullman at **WGBH** draws an analogy between creating a magazine with its cover, table of contents, letters to the editor, and articles, to that of a television program like ***Columbus and the Age of Discovery.*** In both cases, the designer must find a visual vocabulary to provide common visual features. *Columbus* opens slowly and smoothly, establishing a time and a place. A ship rocking on the waves becomes a kind of "wallpaper" on which to show credits. The opening is a reference to what happened—it speaks of ships, ocean, New World, Earth—without actually telling the story.

In contrast, the computer-graphic map sequences are **technical animation** and a critical part of the storytelling. Was Columbus correct in his vision of the

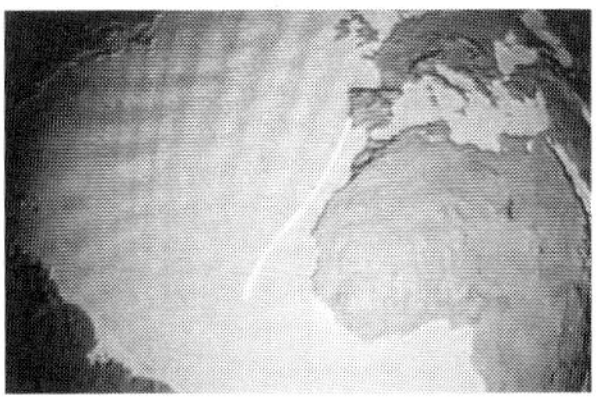

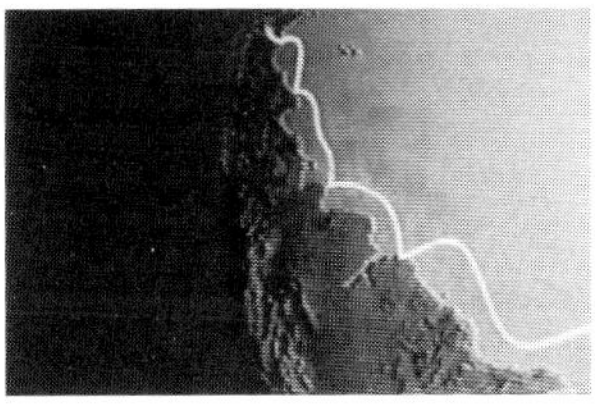

landmass west of Europe? Something was there, but what and how big? Was it the Asian landmass Columbus had promised to find? In 1516, Magellan sailed around the Americas by rounding Cape Horn—and found 5,000 more miles of sea travel to Japan! Columbus had made a colossal miscalculation.

The designer needed to **visualize** this error. Authentic ancient maps established the perspective of the past; computer animation provided the story as we understand it today and extended the viewer's perspective with a three-dimensional presentation. Pullman created a 3-D data base with light source and ocean detail for this fifty-seven-second sequence. "The move was designed to follow the retreating edge of darkness, as the sun revealed the vastness of the Pacific Ocean and the delicate track of Magellan's expedition snaked west. As the Pacific finally fills the whole frame, the music, narration, and camera work conspire to create that one goose-bump moment. In video, **choreography,** not composition, is the essential skill."

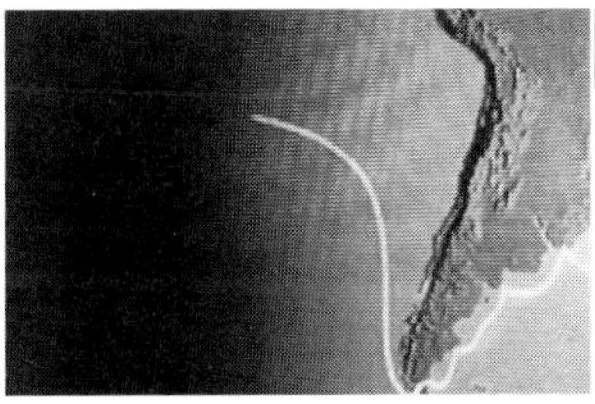

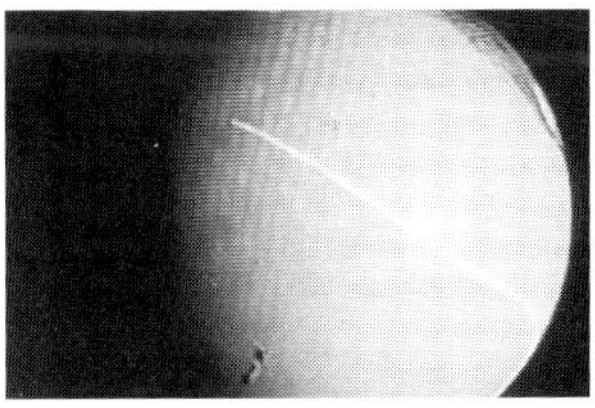

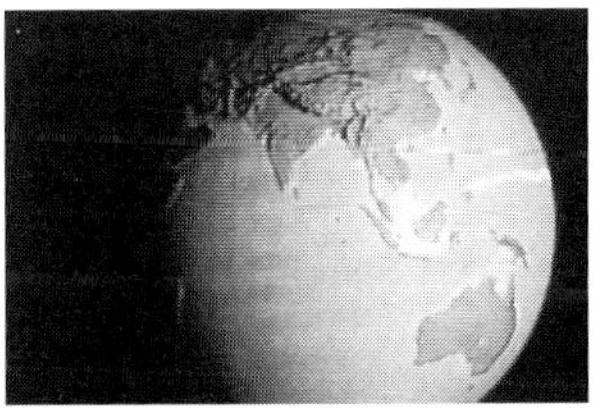

Even as an adolescent, I was interested in "applied art." I was attracted to the combination of "art" (drawing, painting, etc.) and its practical application. While there was no established profession at the time (or certainly none that I knew of), my eyes were opened by the Friend-Heftner book *Graphic Design* and my taste more fully formed under a group of talented teachers in graduate school. I still enjoy the challenge of problem solving.
Tom Geismar

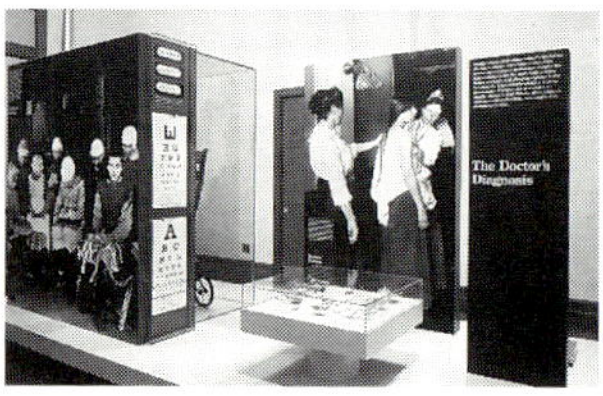

Exhibit Design

Objects, statistics, documentary photographs, labels, lighting, text and headlines, color, space, and place— these are the materials of exhibition design. The designer's problem is how to frame these materials with a storyline that engages and informs an audience and makes the story come alive. **The Ellis Island Immigration Museum** provides an example of how exhibition designers solve such a problem.

The museum at Ellis Island honors the many thousands of immigrants who passed through this processing center on their way to becoming United States citizens. It also underscores our diversity as a nation. The **story** is told from two perspectives: the personal quest for a better life, which focuses on individuals and families, and the mass migration itself, a story of epic proportions.

Tom Geismar wanted to evoke a strong sense of the people who moved through the spaces of Ellis Island. In the entry to the baggage room, he used **space** as a **dramatic** device to ignite the viewer's curiosity. Using a

Exhibit Design
Chermayeff & Geismar, Inc.
Established 1960
New York City

coarse screen like that used in old newspapers, Geismar enlarged old photographs to life size and then mounted these transparent images on glass. The result is an open space in which ghostly people from the past seem to appear.

The problem of how to dramatize statistical information was another challenge. The exhibit *Where We Came From: Sources of Immigration* uses three-dimensional bar **charts** to show the number of people coming from various continents in twenty-year intervals; the height of the vertical element signals volume. *The Peopling of America,* a thematic flag of one thousand faces, shows Americans today. The faces are mounted on two sides of a **prism;** the third side of the prism is an American flag. This striking design becomes a focal point for the visitor and is retained as a powerful **memory.**

Exhibit design creates a story in space. Designers who work in this field tend to enjoy **complexity** and are skilled in composition and visual framing, model making, and the use of diagrams, graphics, and maps.

Signage Design

As people become more mobile—exploring different countries, cities, sites, and buildings—complex signage design helps them locate their destinations and work out a travel plan. One large and multifaceted tourist attraction that recently revamped its signage design is the world-famous **Louvre Museum,** in Paris, France. In addition to the complexity of the building and its art collection, language and cultural differences proved to be fundamental design problems in developing a signage system for the Louvre.

Design simply provided the broadest range of creative opportunities. It also appealed to my personal interest in two- and three-dimensional work including everything from a simple poster to a major exhibit.
Ken Carbone

Carbone Smolan Associates was invited to compete for this project sponsored by the French government. In his proposal, Carbone emphasized his team's credentials, their philosophy regarding signage projects, and their conceptual approach to working on **complex projects.** Carbone Smolan Associates won the commission because they were sensitive to French culture, they were the only competitor to ask questions, and their proposal was unique in developing **scenarios** for how museum visitors would actually use the signage system.

Signage Design
Carbone Smolan Assoc.
Established 1977
New York City

The seventeenth-century Louvre, with its strikingly modern metal-and-glass entryway designed in the 1980s, presented a **visual contrast** of classicism and modernity. Should the signage harmonize with the past or emphasize the present? The design solution combines Granjon, a seventeenth-century French typeface, with contemporary graphics.

The signage design also had to address an internal **navigational problem:** how would visitors find their way through the various buildings? To add to the potential confusion, art collections are often moved around within the museum. The designers came up with an **innovative plan:** they created "neighborhoods" within the Louvre, neighborhoods that remained the same regardless of the collection currently in place. The signage identified the specific neighborhoods; the design elements of a printed guide (available in five languages) related each neighborhood to a particular Louvre environment. It's clear that signage designers need skills in design systems and planning as well as in diagramming and model making.

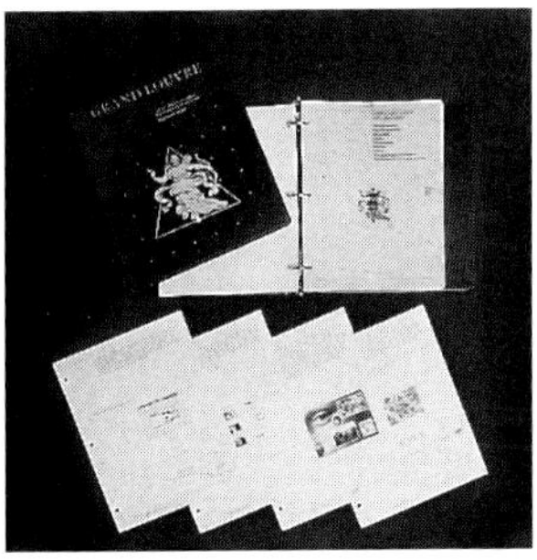

Package Design

Packaging performs many functions: it protects, stores, displays, announces a product's identity, promotes, and sometimes instructs. But today, given increased **environmental concern** and waste-recycling needs, packaging has come under scrutiny. The functions packaging has traditionally performed remain; what is needed now is environmentally responsive design. Fitch Richardson Smith developed just such a design—really an **"un-packaging"** strategy—for the Gardena line of watering products.

A less-is-more strategy was ideally suited to capture the loyalty of an **environmentally aware consumer**—a gardener. The designers' approach was to eliminate individual product packaging by using sturdy, corrugated, precut shipping bins as point-of-purchase displays. Hangtags on individual products were designed to answer the customer's questions at point-of-sale and to be saved for use-and-care instructions at home. This approach cut

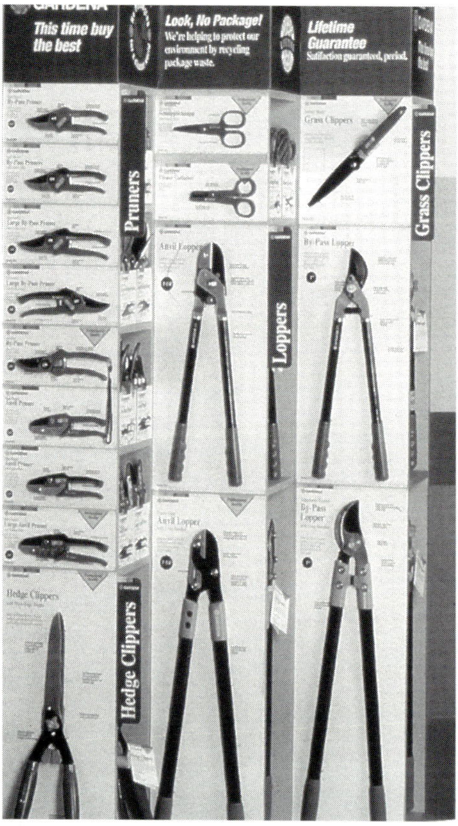

costs and reduced environmental impact in both manufacturing and consumption. What's more, Gardena discovered that customers liked being able to **touch** and hold the products before purchase.

Retailers report that this merchandising system reduces space needs, permits tailoring of the product assortment, and minimizes the burden on the sales staff. A **modular system,** it is expandable and adaptable and can be presented freestanding or on shelves or pegboards. The **graphics** are clear, bright, and logical, reinforcing the systematic approach to merchandising and information design. Contemporary environmental values are clearly expressed in this packaging solution. The product connects with consumers who care about their gardens, and the packaging-design solution relates to their concern about the Earth.

Package designers tend to have a strong background in three-dimensional design, design and product management, and design systems.

Environmental Design

Environmental graphics establish a particular sense of place through the use of two- and three-dimensional forms, graphics, and signage. The **1984 Olympics** is an interesting example of a project requiring this kind of design treatment. The different communication needs of the various Olympics participants—athletes, officials, spectators, support crews, and television viewers—together with the project's brief use, combined to create an environmental-design problem of daunting dimension and complexity.

In the 1984 Los Angeles Games, the focus was on how a **multicultural** American city could embrace an **international** event. Arrangements were basic and low-budget. Events, planned to be cost-conscious and inclusive, were integrated into Los Angeles rather than isolated from it. Old athletic stadiums were retrofitted rather than replaced with new ones. These ideas and values, as well as the celebratory, international nature of the Olympics, needed to be **expressed** in its environmental design.

Environmental Design
Sussman/Prejza and Company
Established 1968
Los Angeles

One of the most important considerations was to design a **visual system** that would provide identity and unity for individual events that were scattered throughout an existing urban environment. Through the use of color and light, the visual system highlighted the geographic and climatic connection between Los Angeles and the Mediterranean environment of the original Greek Games. The graphics expressed celebration, while the three-dimensional physical forms were a kind of "instant architecture"—sonotubes, scaffolding, and existing surfaces were signed and painted with the visual system. The **clarity** and **exuberance** of the system brought the pieces together in a cohesive, immediately recognizable way.

Under the direction of Sussman/Prejza, the design took form in workshops and warehouses all over the city. **Logistics**—the physical scope of the design and the time required for its development and installation—demanded that the designers exhibit not only skill with images, symbols, signs, and model making but also considerable design-planning expertise.

Larry Keeley is a *design planner.* He helps companies use many different kinds of design to create important innovations.

Design Planning

Strategic design planners are interested in the **big picture.** They help clients create innovation throughout an industry rather than in one individually designed object or communication. First, the strategic design planners develop a **point of view** about what the client needs to do. Then they **orchestrate** the use of a wide variety of design specialities. The end result integrates these **specialities** into an entire vision for the client and the customer. This approach unites business goals, such as customer satisfaction or increasing market share, with specific design performance.

The scope of strategic design planning is illustrated by one Doblin Group project. Customer satisfaction was the goal of the **Amoco Customer-Driven Facility.** Larry Keeley, a strategic design planner at the Doblin Group, relates that "the idea was to reconceive the **nature** of the gas station. And like many design programs, this one began with a rough sketch that suggested how gas stations might **function** very differently." The design team needed to go beyond giving Amoco a different "look." They needed to

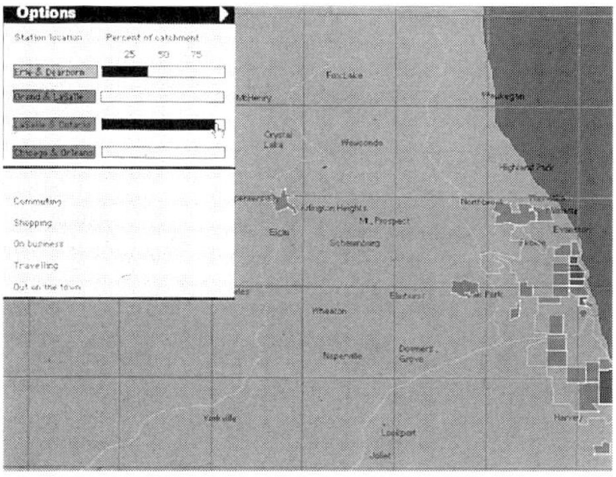

consider customer behavior, the quality of the job for employees, the kinds of fuel the car of the future might use, and thousands of other details. Everything was to be built around the convenience and comfort of **customers.**

Keeley and his team collaborated with other design and engineering firms to analyze, **prototype,** and **pilot-test** the design. The specific outcomes of the project include developments that are not often associated with graphic design. For example, the project developed new construction materials as well as station-operation methods that are better for the environment and the customer. A gas nozzle that integrates the display of dispensed gas with a fume-containment system was also developed. This system was designed to be particularly user-friendly to handicapped or elderly customers. For Amoco itself, software-planning tools were developed to help the company decide where to put gas stations so that they become good neighbors. These new kinds of **gas stations** are now in operation and are a success.

Publication Systems

Creating a visual system is like designing a game. You need to ask: What is the purpose? What are the key elements and relationships? What are the rules? And where are the opportunities for surprise? With over 350 national parks and millions of visitors, the **United States National Park Service** (NPS) needed a publication system to help visitors orient themselves no matter which park they were in, to understand the geological or historical significance of the park, and to better access its recreational opportunities. The parts of the system had to work individually and as a whole.

Systems design involves considerations of **user needs,** communication consistency, design processes, production requirements, and economies of scale, including the standardization of sizes. Rather than examining and designing an isolated piece, the designer of a system considers the whole, abstracting its requirements and essential elements to form a kind of **game plan** for the creation of its parts. When Massimo Vignelli was hired to

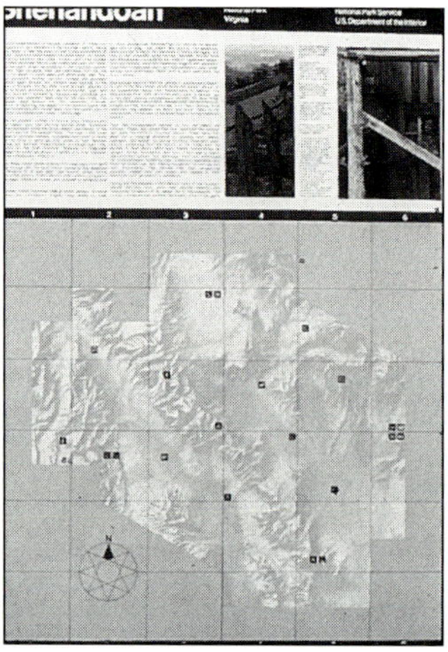

Publication Systems
Vignelli Associates
Established 1971
New York City

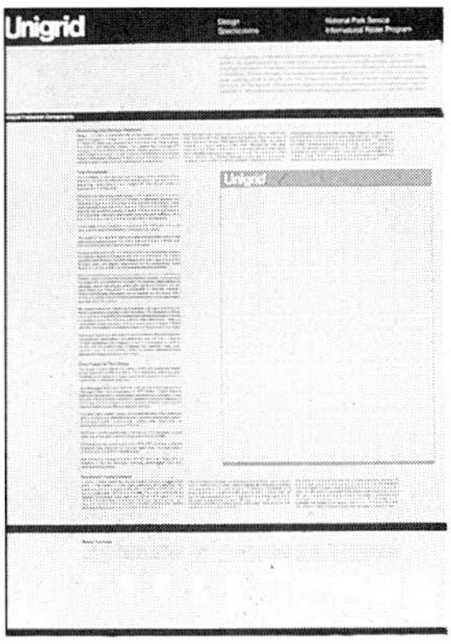

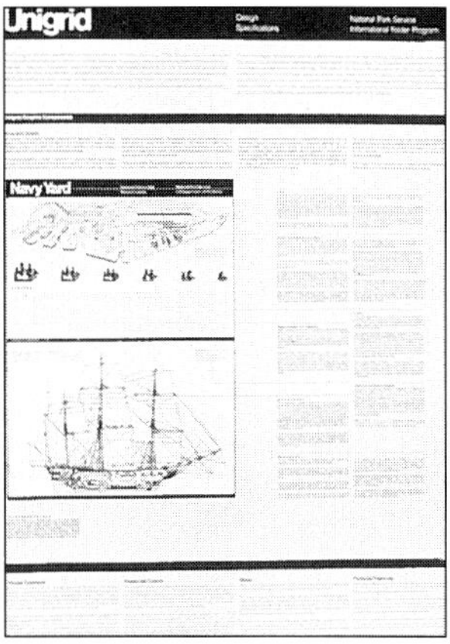

work with the NPS design staff, they agreed on a publication system with six elements: a limited set of formats; full-sheet presentations; park names used as logotypes; horizontal organization for text, maps, and images; standardized, open, asymmetric typographic layout; and a master grid to coordinate design with printing. The system supports simple, bold graphics like *Liberty* or detailed information like *Shenandoah Park,* with its relief map, text, and photographs.

A well-conceived system is not a straightjacket; it leaves room for **imaginative solutions.** It releases the designer from solving the same problem again and again and directs creative energy to the unique aspects of a communication. To remain vital and current, the system must anticipate problems *and* opportunities. Designers working in this area need design-planning skills as well as creativity with text, images, symbols, signs, diagrams, graphs, and maps.

Educational Design

Educational publishing isn't just textbooks anymore. Traditional materials are now joined by a number of new options. Because children and teenagers grow up with television and computers, they are accustomed to **interactive experiences.** This, plus the fact that students learn best in different ways—some by eye and some by ear—makes educational publishing an important challenge for design.

Ligature believes that combining visual and verbal learning components in a cooperative, creative environment is of paramount importance in developing educational materials. Ligature uses considerate instructional design, incorporating fine art, illustrations, and diagrams, to produce educational products that are engaging, substantive, relevant, and effective.

A recent Ligature project for a middle school language arts curriculum presents twelve thematic units in **multiple ways:** as a full-color magazine, a paperback

A young painter sets up an easel in her kitchen and finds inspiration in the groceries sitting on the counter. A twelve-year-old girl reads books about braille and is moved to create software for people who can't speak or write. A poet lets ideas surface from the dreamlike state that begins his day. A fifteenth-century genius designs machines that can't be produced until the twentieth century. The creative spirit is fuelled by different sparks and revealed in different ways. Enter the world of Creativity, and see how people from all around the world express their unique feelings and ideas.

"When the generals are forgotten, when the monuments have crumbled, what still lives is the work of the artist—the words, the movements, the feeling, and the music."

—LIV ULLMANN

Unfortunately, too many people think that creativity is something mysterious that only belongs to certain people, whereas everyone has access to it.

—John Cage

Genius is one percent inspiration and ninety-nine percent perspiration.

—Thomas Alva Edison

Imagination is more important than knowledge.

All music is creation. It is one of the most mysterious and deeply moving experiences you can have.

—LEONARD BERNSTEIN

4 CREATIVITY CREATIVITY 5

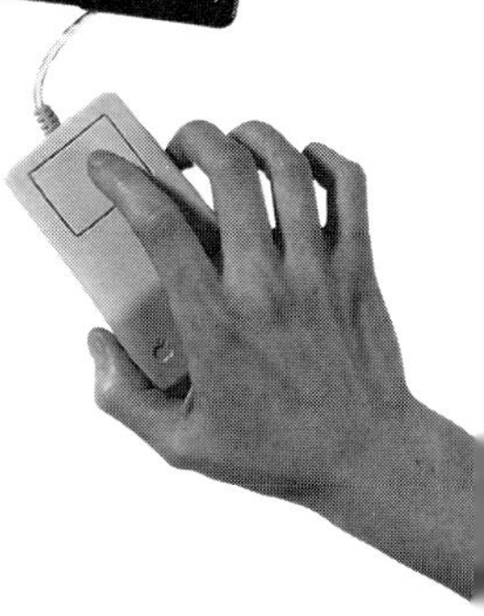

anthology, an audiotape, several videotapes, a language arts survival guide giving instruction on writing, software, fine art transparencies, and a teacher's guide containing suggestions for integrating these materials. These rich **learning resources** encourage creativity on the part of both teachers and students and allow a more interactive approach to learning.

Middle school students are in transition from child to adult. The central design issue was to create materials that look youthful but not childish, that are fresh, fun, and lively, yet look "grown up." The anthology has few illustrations and looks very adult, while the magazine uses type and many lively images as design elements.

In educational publishing, multidisciplinary creative teams use prototype testing to explore new ideas. Materials are also **field-tested** on teachers and students. Designers going into instructional systems development need to be interested in information, communication, planning, and **teamwork.**

Magazine Design

What makes you pick up a particular magazine? What do you look at first? What keeps you turning the pages? In general, your answers probably involve some combination of content (text) and design (images, typography, and other graphic elements). Magazine designers ask those same questions for every issue they work on; then they try to imagine the answers of their own particular **audience**—their slice of the magazine market.

At ***Rolling Stone,*** designers work in conjunction with the art director, editors, and photo editors to add a **"visual voice"** to the text. They think carefully about their audience and use a variety of images and typefaces to keep readers interested. "We try to pull the reader in with unique and lively opening pages and follow through with turnpages that have a good balance of photos and pullquotes to keep the reader interested," says deputy art director Gail Anderson. Designers also select typefaces that suggest the appropriate mood for each story.

The designers work on their features from conception to execution, **consulting** with **editors** to help determine the amount of space that each story needs. They also

work with the copy and **production** departments on text changes, letterspacing, type, and the sizing of art. At the beginning of the two-week cycle, designers start with printouts of feature stories. They select photographs and design a headline. Over the course of the next two to three days, they design the layouts. At the same time, each *Rolling Stone* designer is responsible for one or more of the magazine's departments and lays out those pages as well. Eventually both editors and designers sign off on various stages of the production process and examine final proofs.

Anderson is excited about how the new **technology** has changed the role of magazine designers. "We now have the freedom to set and design type ourselves, to experiment with color and see the results instantly, and to work in what feels like 3-D. The designer's role has certainly expanded, and I think it is taken more seriously than it was even a few years ago." Magazine designers should enjoy working with both type and images, be attuned to content concerns and able to work well with editors, have technological expertise, and be able to tolerate tight **deadlines.**

Illustration

Drawing—deciding what is significant detail, what can be suggested, and what needs dramatic development—is a skill that all designers need in order to develop their own ideas and share them with others. Many designers use **drawing** as the core of their work. Milton Glaser is such a designer.

Keeping a creative edge and searching for new opportunities for visual development are important aspects of a lively design practice. When Glaser felt an urge to **expand** his drawing vocabulary and to do more personally satisfying work, he found himself attracted to the impressionist artist Claude Monet. Glaser liked the way Monet looked: his physical characteristics expressed something familiar and yet mysterious. Additionally, Monet's **visual vocabulary** was foreign to Glaser whose work is more linear and graphic. While many designers would be intimidated by Monet's stature in the art world, Glaser was not because he was consciously

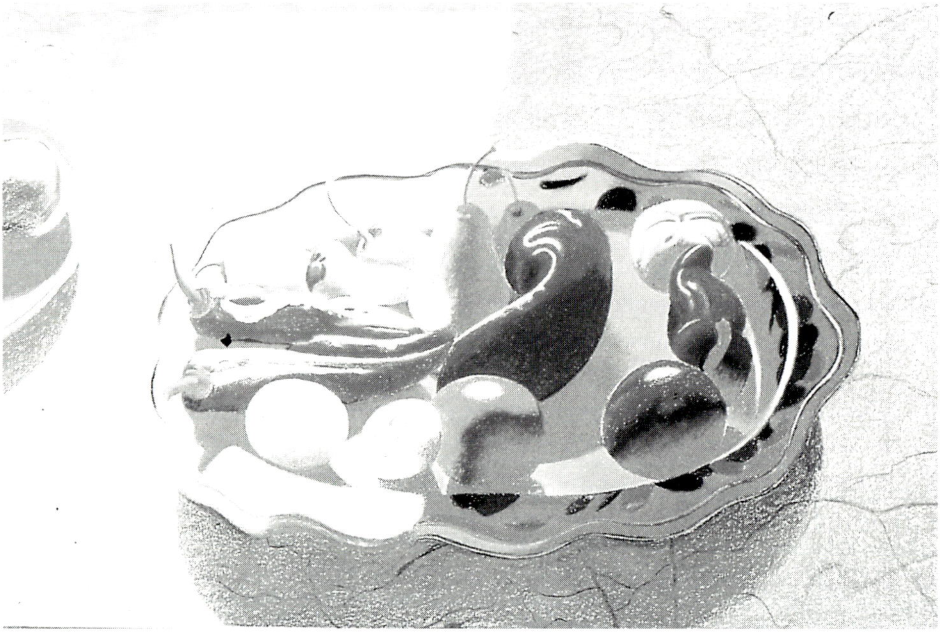

Illustration
Milton Glaser, Inc.
Established 1974
New York City

seeking an opportunity for visual growth. In a sense, Glaser's drawings of Monet were a lark—an invention done lightly.

Glaser worked directly from nature, from photographs, and from memory in order to open himself to new possibilities. The drawings, forty-eight in all, were done over a year and a half and then were shown in a gallery in Milan. They became the catalog for a local printer who wanted to demonstrate his color fidelity and excellence in printing. The drawings demonstrate the designer's **flexibility** of vision: the selection of detail, the balancing of light and shadow, and the varying treatments of figure and background. The drawing below, with its **attention** to background, in a sense shows what Monet sees.

Drawing is a rich and immediate way to represent the world, but drawing can also illustrate ideas in partnership with design.

Identity Design

Creating the **key graphic element** that identifies a product or service and separates it from its competitors is a challenging design problem. The identity needs to be clear and memorable. It should be adaptable to extreme changes in scale, from a matchbox to a large illuminated sign. And it must embody the **character** and **quality** of what it identifies. This capturing of an intangible is an important feature of identity design, but it is also a subtle talent.

Hotel Hankyu International is the flagship hotel for the Hankyu Corporation, a huge, diversified Japanese company. It is relatively small for a luxury hotel, with only six floors of accomodations. The client wanted to establish the hotel as an international hotel, rather than a Japanese hotel. In Japan, "international" means European or American. Consequently, the client did not look to Japanese designers, but they hired Pentagram—with the understanding that the hotel's emblem would be a flower, since flowers are universally associated with pleasure.

HOTEL HANKYU INTERNATIONAL

HOTEL HANKYU INTERNATIONAL

The identity was commissioned first, before other visual decisions (such as those about the interior architecture) were made. Here the graphic designer could set the visual agenda. Rather than one flower, **six flowers** were designed as the identity, one for each floor. To differentiate itself in its market, this small luxury hotel benefited from an extravagant design. Each flower is made up of four lines that emerge from the base of a square. The flowers are reminiscent of the 1920s Art Deco period, which suggests sophistication and world travel. Color and **related typefaces** link the flowers. One typeface is a custom-designed, slim Roman alphabet with proportions similar to those of the flowers. The other consists of Japanese characters and was designed by a Japanese firm.

The identity appears on signage, room folders, stationery, packaging, and other hotel amenities. It is clear and **memorable** and conveys a sense of luxury. Designers working with identity design need to be skilled manipulators of **visual abstraction,** letterforms, and design systems.

Designers are problem solvers who create solutions regardless of the medium. But, designers create within the confines of reality. The challenge is to push the limits of reality to achieve the most effective solution.
Lorena Cummings

Systems Design

Systems design seeks to unify and coordinate all aspects of a complex communication. It strives to achieve consistent verbal and visual treatment and to reduce production time and cost. Systems design requires a careful **problem-solving** approach to handling complexity.

Caterpillar Inc. is a worldwide heavy-equipment and engine manufacturer. Its most visible and highly used document is the *Specalog*, a product-information book containing specifications, sales and marketing information, and a competitive-product reference list. A *Specalog* is produced for each of fifty different product types in twenty-six languages. The catalog output totals seventy million pages annually. Before Siegel & Gale took on *Specalog*, no formal **guidelines** existed, so the pages took too much time to create and were inconsistent with Caterpillar's literature strategy and corporate image.

Bringing systematic order and clarity to this mountain of information was Siegel & Gale's task. First they asked questions: What do customers and dealers need to know?

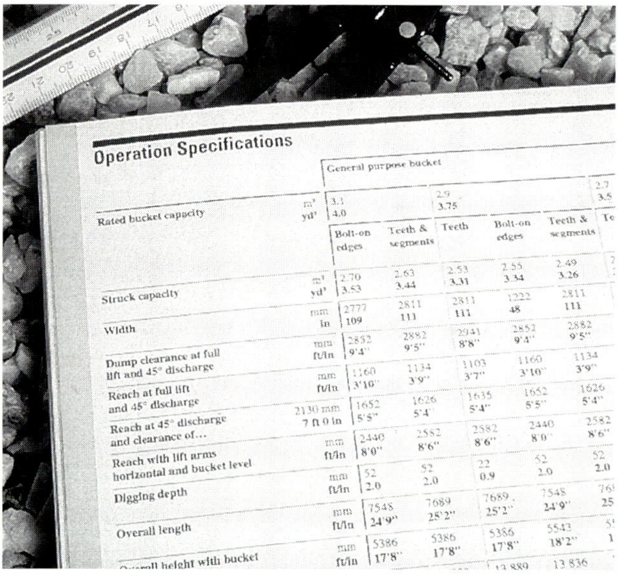

What do the information producers (Caterpillar's product units) want? An analysis of existing *Specalogs* revealed problems with both verbal and visual language: there was no clear **organization** for content; language was generic; product images were taken from too great a distance; and specifications charts lacked typographic clarity. The brochures of Caterpillar's competitors were also analyzed so as not to miss opportunities to make *Specalog* distinctive. These activities resulted in a clear set of **design goals.**

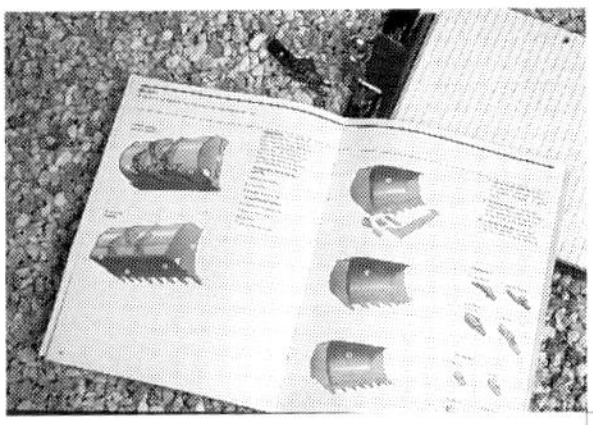

A working **prototype** was tested with customers and dealers. Following revisions, the new design was implemented worldwide. Its significant features include an easy-to-use template system compatible with existing Macintosh computers (thus allowing for local-market customization), a thirty-percent saving in production time and cost, and increased approval by both customers and dealers. Achieving standardization while encouraging customization is a strategy in many large international organizations. Designers involved with projects like this study information design, design planning, and evaluation techniques.

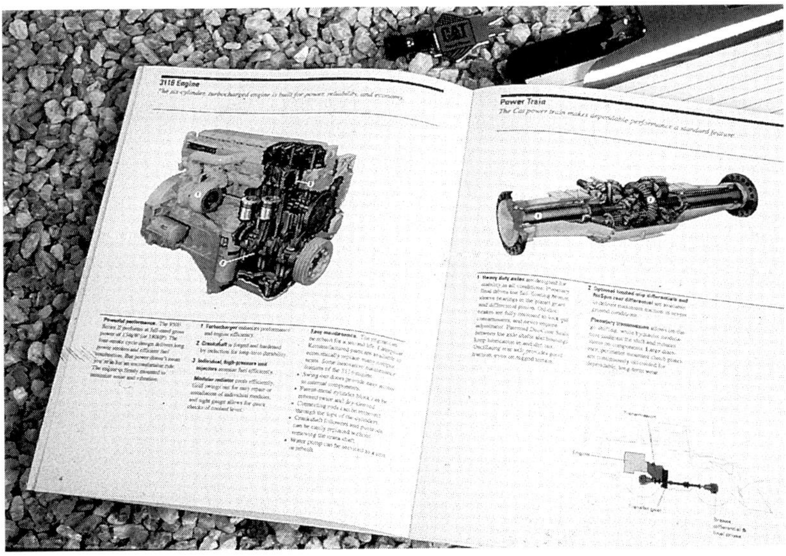

My early exposure to a design studio made me aware of the design profession as an opportunity to apply analytical abilities to an interest in the fine arts. Graduate design programs made it possible for me to delve more deeply into the aspects of design I found personally interesting. Since then, the nature of the design profession, which constantly draws the designer into a wide range of subjects and problems, has continued to interest me in each new project. It's been this opportunity to satisfy personal interests while earning a living that has made design my long-term career choice.
Won Chung

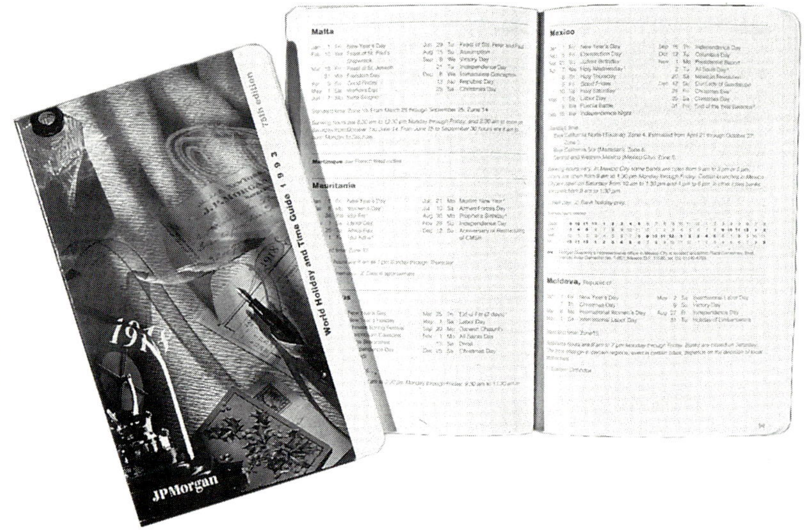

Corporate Communication

Whether they are large or small, corporations need to remind their public who they are, what they are doing, and how well they are doing it. Even the venerable Wall Street banking firm of **J. P. Morgan** needs to assert itself so the public remembers its existence and service. Corporate communications serve this function, and the design of these messages goes a long way toward establishing company image.

Usually corporate communications include identity programs and annual reports, but there are also other opportunities to communicate the corporate message. Since 1918, J. P. Morgan has published a **unique guide** that keeps up with the changing world of commerce and travel. *The World Holiday and Time Guide* covers over two hundred countries, and keeps the traveler current with twenty-four time zones. In the *Guide,* the international businessperson can find easy-to-read tables and charts giving the banking hours as well as opening and closing business times for weekdays and holidays. Specific

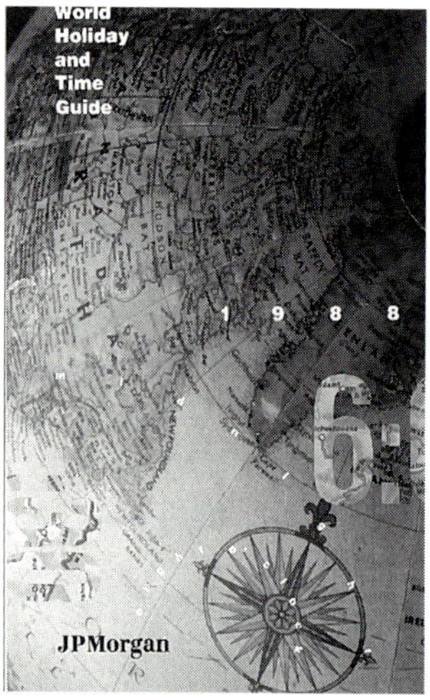

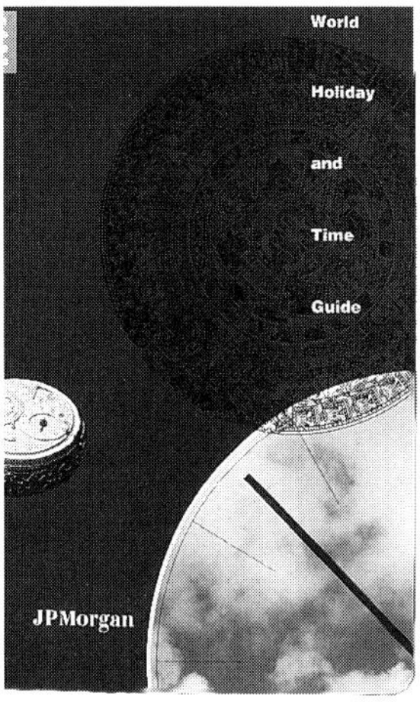

Corporate Communication
J. P. Morgan & Company, Corporate Communication
Established 1982
New York City

cultural holidays, such as Human Rights Day (December 10) in Namibia and National Tree Planting Day (March 23) in Lesotho are included. The seventy-five-year history of the *Guide* is also an informal chronicle of world change. It has described the rise and decline of Communism and the liberation of colonial Africa and Asia; today it keeps up with the recent territorial changes in Europe. The covers of the *Guide* invite the user to **celebrate** travel and cultural diversity; the interior format is a model of **clarity** and convenience.

In-house design groups have two functions: they provide a design service for their company and they maintain the corporate image. Because projects are often annual, responsibility for them moves around the design group, helping to sustain **creativity** and to generate a fresh approach to communication. Consequently, the *Guide* is the work of several designers. To work in corporate communications, designers need skills relating to typography, **information design,** and print design.

I like the way words look, the way ideas can become things. I like the social, activist, practical, and aesthetic aspects of design.
Laurie Haycock Makela

Nonprofit Design

Just as profit-oriented corporations need to present a carefully defined visual identity to their public, so must a nonprofit organization like the **Walker Art Center.** Even with limited resources, this museum uses graphic designers to present its best face to the public.

For twenty years the Walker Art Center presented itself in a quiet, restrained, and neutral manner. It was a model of contemporary corporate graphics. But times change, and like many American museums, the Walker is now taking another look at its role in society. The questions the Walker is considering include: What kind of museum is this? Who is its audience? How does the museum tell its story to its audience? What should its visual identity and publications look like? **Identity** builds expectation. Does the identity established by the museum's communications really support the programs the Walker offers?

The stock-in-trade of the Walker Art Center includes exhibitions and the performing arts for audiences ranging

Nonprofit Design
Walker Art Center
Established 1963
Minneapolis, Minnesota

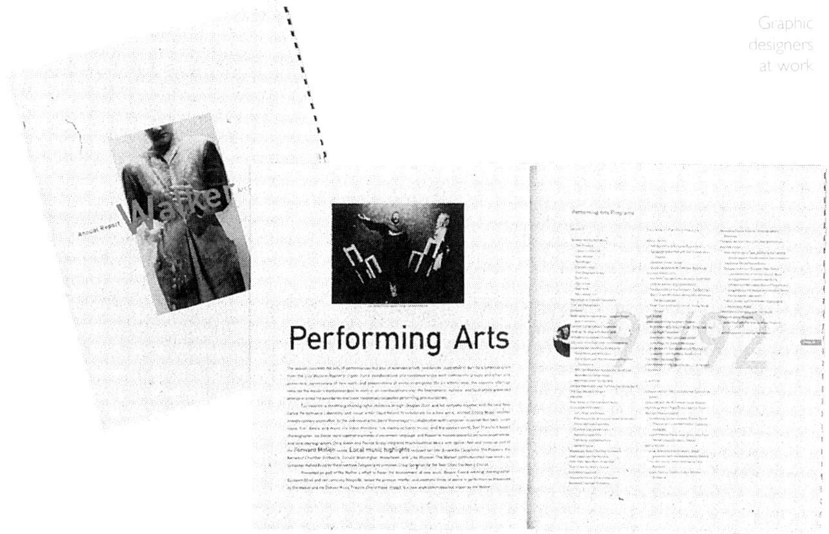

from children to scholars, educational programs, and avant-garde programming in film and video. As the museum's programming becomes even more varied, the old "corporate" identity represented by a clean, utilitarian design no longer seems appropriate. To better represent the expanded range of art and audience at the museum, The Design Studio, an internal laboratory for design experimentation at the Walker, is purposely blurring aspects of high and low culture and using more **experimental** typefaces and more **eclectic** communication approaches. Posters, catalogs, invitations to exhibitions, and mailers for film and performing arts programs often have independent design and typographic approaches, while the calendar and members' magazine provide a continuity of design.

Publication design, symbol and identity systems, and type and image relationships are among the areas of expertise necessary for in-house museum designers.

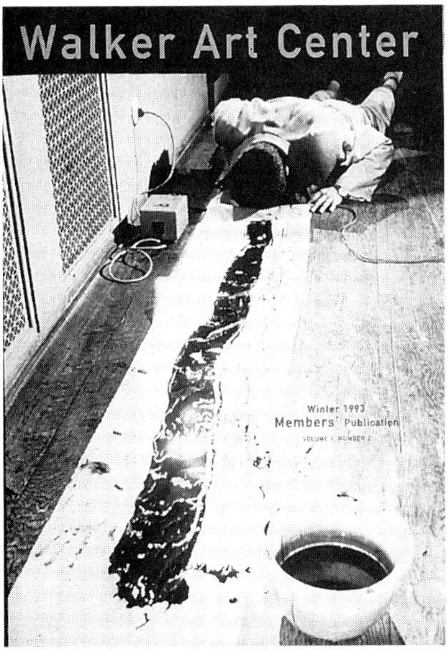

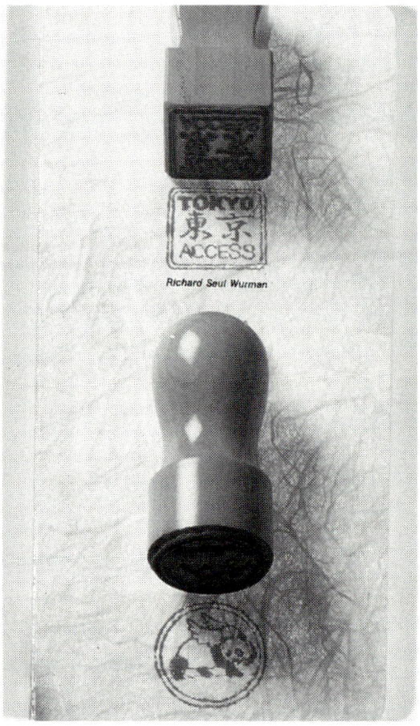

Information Design

How do you get around in an unfamiliar city? What if the language is completely different from English? What kind of guidebook can help you bridge the communication gap? ***Access Tokyo*** is a successful travel guide to one of the most complex cities in the world. It is also an example of information design, the goal of which is **clarity** and **usefulness.**

Richard Wurman began the Tokyo project as an innocent, without previous experience in that city. His challenge was to see if he could understand enough about Tokyo to make major decisions about what to include in a guidebook. He also needed to develop useful instructions to help the English-speaking tourist get around. Ignorance (lack of information) and intelligence (knowing how to find that information) led him to ask the questions that brought **insight** and **order** to his project. Using his skill in information and book design, the designer used his own experience as a visitor to translate the experience of Tokyo for others.

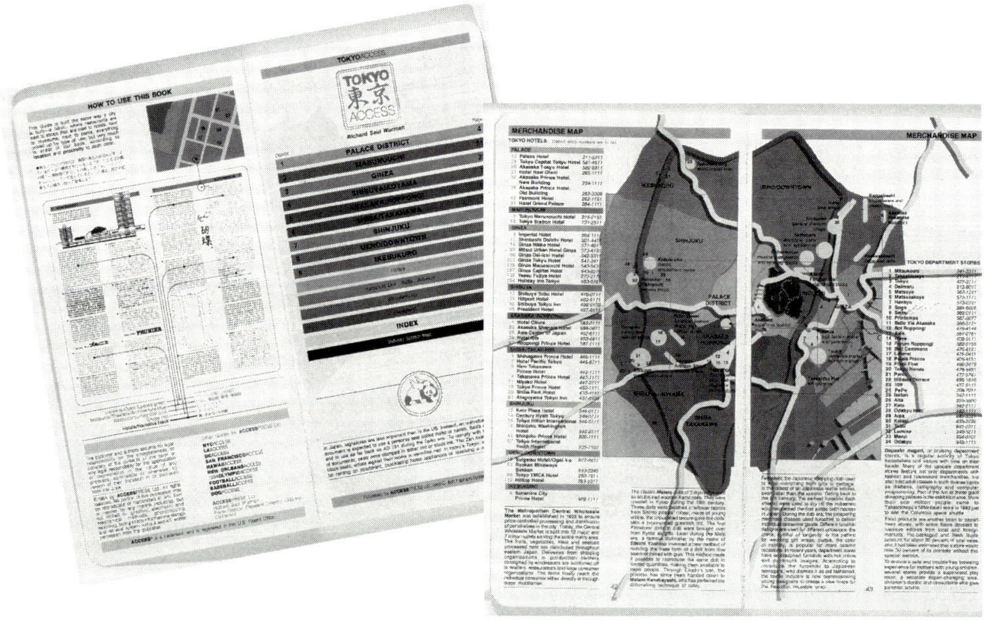

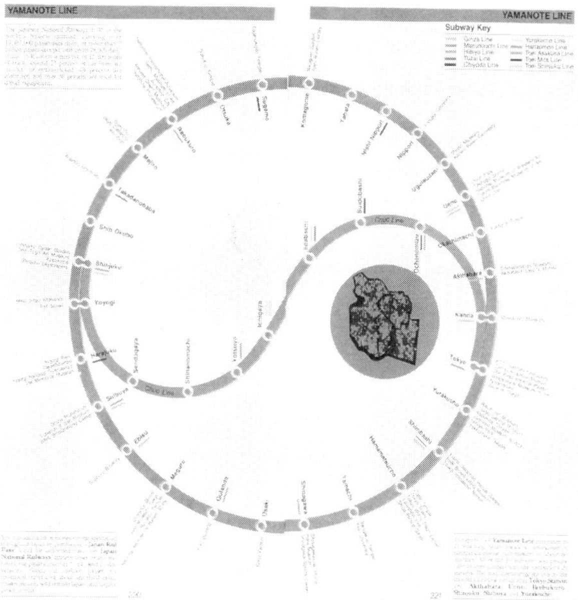

Access Tokyo presents the historical, geographical, and cultural qualities that make Tokyo unique, as well as resources and locations for the outsider. **Maps** are a particular challenge since they require reducing information to its essential structure. The map for the Yamanote Line, a subway that rings Tokyo, is clear and memorable. The guide is **bilingual** because of the language gap between English with its Roman alphabet and Japanese with its ideographic signs. The traveler can read facts of interest in English but can also show the Japanese translation to a cab driver.

Wurman also wanted to get the cultural viewpoint across. To this end, he asked Japanese architects, painters, and designers to contribute **graphics** to the project. The colorful tangram (a puzzle made by cutting a square of paper into five triangles, a square, and a rhomboid) is abstract in a very Japanese way. *Access Tokyo* bridges the **culture** chasm as well as the information gap.

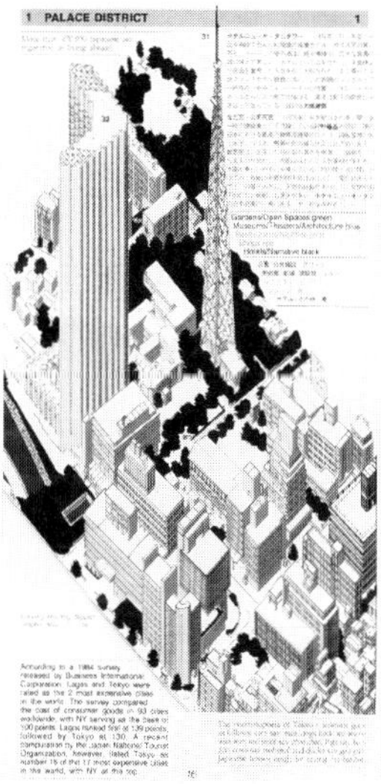

I became a designer by accident; it was less boring than working in a store.

I do have some regrets, however, as I would prefer to be in control of content rather than form.
Tibor Kalman

Design Entrepreneur

"One who organizes, manages, and assumes the risks of a business enterprise . . ." This dictionary definition of the word *entrepreneur* is a bland description of a very interesting possibility in design. A design entrepreneur extends the general definition: he or she must have a particular **vision** of an object and its market. While many designers believe they could be their own best client, few act on this notion. Tibor Kalman of M&Co. has acted: he is a design entrepreneur.

Kalman's firm, M&Co., is not without clients in the usual sense. Their innovative graphics for the Talking Heads music video "(Nothing but) Flowers" demonstrates that **creativity** and even **fun** are possible in traditional design work for clients. But somehow this wasn't enough for Kalman. He was frustrated with doing the packaging, advertising, and promotion for things he often viewed critically. He wanted to do the "real thing," the object itself.

Kalman started with a **traditional object,** a wristwatch. He then applied his own particular sense of humor and elegant restraint to the "ordinary" watch in order to examine formal ideas about time. The *Pie* watch gives only a segment, or slice, of time, while the *Ten One 4* wristwatch is such a masterpiece of understatement that it is in the permanent design collection of the Museum of Modern Art. Other variations include *Romeo* (with Roman numerals rather than Arabic ones), *Straphanger* (with the face rotated ninety degrees to accommodate easy reading on the subway), and *Bug* (with bugs substituted for the usual numerals). These few examples give a sense of the wry **humor** that transforms an ordinary object into a unique personal pleasure.

Entrepreneurial design requires creativity and **business savvy** along with design and project-management skills. Of course, an innovative concept is also a necessity. Vision and **risk-taking** are important attributes for the design entrepreneur.

Corporate Executive

If you are a take-charge person with **vision,** creativity, and communication and organizational skills, becoming a design executive might be a good long-term career goal. Obviously, no one starts out with this job; it takes years to grow into it. A brief review of Robert Blaich's career can illustrate what being a design executive is all about.

Educated as an architect, Blaich became involved with marketing when he joined Herman Miller, a major American furniture maker. Then he assumed a product-planning role and began to consciously build design talent for the organization. By the time he was vice president of design and communication, Blaich was running Herman Miller's entire design program (including communication, product, and architectural design). In a sense, he was their **total designer.**

In 1980 Blaich came to Philips Electronics N.V., an international manufacturer of entertainment and

Corporate Executive Philips Electronics NV Design Department Established 1923 Eindhoven, The Netherlands

information systems. Located in the Netherlands, Philips is the world's twenty-eighth largest corporation and was seen by many Americans as a stodgy foreign giant. The president of Philips asked Blaich to take the corporation in new directions. By the time Blaich left in 1992, design was a **strategic** part of Philips's operation, and its dull image was reinvigorated and **unified.** What's more, the corporation now saw its key functions as research, design, manufacturing, marketing, and human resources—in that order. Design's number-two position reflected a new understanding of its importance. Today, as president of Blaich Associates, Blaich is a consultant for Philips and responsible for corporate identity and for strategic notions of design.

Just what do corporate design executives do? They look at design from a business point of view, critique work, support new ideas, foster creativity and collaboration, bring in new talent, and develop new design capabilities. They are **design activists** in a corporate setting.

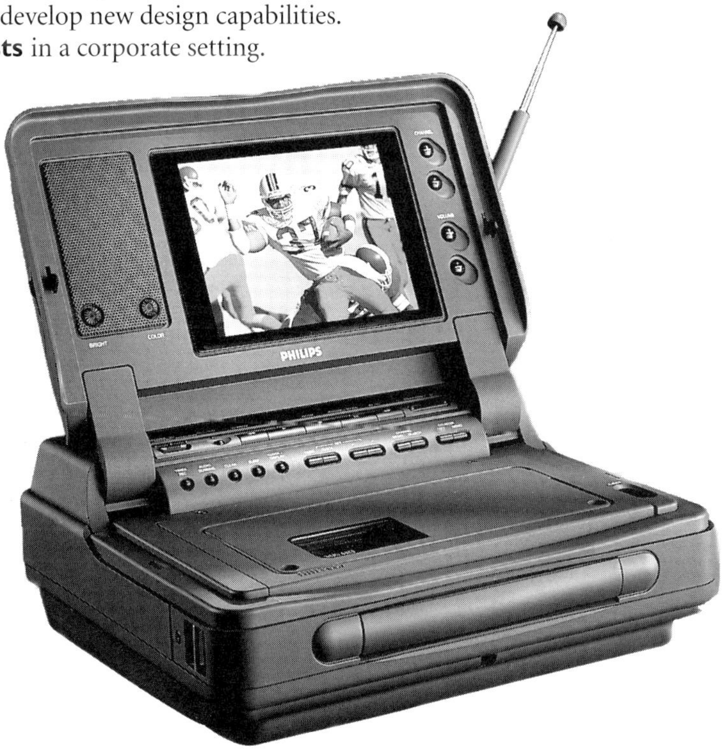

Professor of Design

The best teaching is about learning, exploring, and making connections. **Teachers** in professional programs are almost never exclusively educators; they also **practice design.** Sheila Levrant de Bretteville is a case in point. She is a professor of graphic design at Yale University and owner of The Sheila Studio. Both her teaching and design are geared toward hopeful and inspiriting action.

Looking at a student assignment and at one of de Bretteville's own design projects illuminates the interplay of teaching and practice. De Bretteville saw the windows of abandoned stores in New Haven as an opportunity to communicate across class and color lines. She chose the theme of "grandparents," which formed a connection between her Yale students and the people of the community. The windows became large **posters** that told stories of grandparents as immigrants, as labor leaders, as the very aged, and more. The project gave students the opportunity to explore the requirements of space, materials, and information.

Professor of Design
The Sheila Studio
Established 1970
Hamden, Conn.

Yale University
Established 1950
(Graphic Design)
New Haven, Conn.

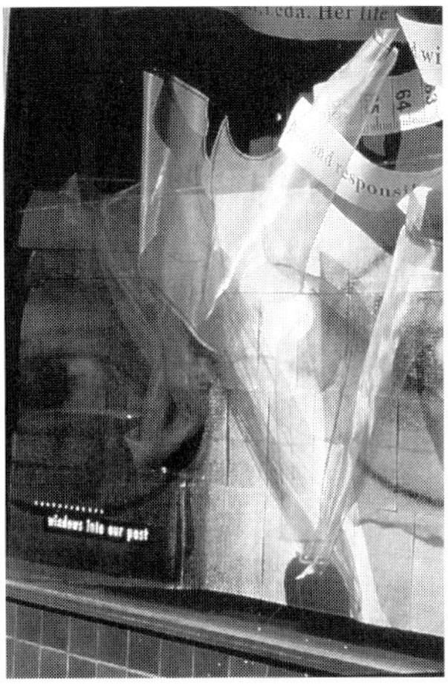

De Bretteville's project, *Biddy Mason: Time and Place,* is an example of **environmental-design.** Located in Los Angeles, it explores the nine decades of Biddy Mason's life: as a slave prior to her arrival in California and as a free woman in Los Angeles where she later lived and worked and founded the AME church. "I wanted to celebrate this woman's perseverance and generosity," says de Bretteville. "Now everyone who comes to this place will know about her and the city that benefitted from her presence here." A designed tactile environment, which included the imperfections in the slate and concrete wall, required working with **processes** and **materials** that were often unpredictable—like the struggles Biddy faced in her life.

Biddy Mason and the grandparent windows **connect** design practice and teaching as de Bretteville encourages her students to use their knowledge, skills, and passion to connect to the community through design.

The Modern Poster
POSTER

What is the future of graphic design?

No book can completely define or describe the field of graphic design. That's because both the practice of graphic design and the education for design careers are constantly changing. As other aspects of society and culture change, so does graphic design. **Clients** develop new products, services, and messages; audiences respond to new styles, symbols, and content; **technology** changes the graphic designer's work. Design **education** not only responds to these changes but also initiates change. The relationship between education and practice is dynamic; innovations in one area lead to new approaches in the other.

Everyone who participated in this book was asked to respond to this question: What future changes do you see for graphic design education or practice? Their answers fall generally into three areas—technological, social, and educational change. How will these **changes affect you,** your choice of career, your education, and your design practice? How can you be prepared? There are no specific answers to these questions—not without a crystal ball. Your best bet is to get a solid background, remain open to new ideas and techniques, and keep an eye on the the world around you. But even more important, you must strive to define your own priorities and develop a particular, personal vision of what it means to be a graphic designer.

Technological Change

From my perspective at WGBH, I see things opening up for designers in nonlinear, nonprint media. Historically, WGBH has thought of itself as a radio/television station, a broadcaster, but now we see ourselves as a publisher but not with traditional methods of distribution. A single theme (like science, or American history) is now multi-versioned into many formats including nonbroadcast, computer-based materials that are interactive and combine live-motion with static print-based materials. The designer is a kind of **middleman for ideas** and needs to move smoothly between media. The traditional designer's skill of merging text and image will continue to be important but in different media applications. The real **fun** in the future will be with **motion and sound.**
Chris Pullman, designer

For a long time, many forms of art have been separated, but now the new media are collapsing disciplines back into one language—sound, motion, image, and text can be reintegrated to portray ideas and life with a richness that can return us to the spirit of things. This is a messy but exciting time—and I am optimistic!

April Greiman, designer

My crystal ball tells me that graphic design in the future will have to do with the characteristics of new media. It will be information-oriented, allowing **form to follow thought;** it will be educational, interactive, spatial and environmental, dynamic and fast, multidisciplinary, collaborative, networked, entertaining, and multicultural.
Roger Remington, educator

Interactive multimedia is moving fast, and designers must become better equipped to work in this area so they can create new design tools for communication. Designers really need to take a hard look at interactive multimedia.
Robert Blaich, designer

Everything will be digital. Recent changes will accelerate, and we will see even more new tools. It will be easier for people who are not designers to visualize things. Before, everything was hard to produce, so there was a level of **abstraction** built into making communications. Now the danger is that the technology lets you become **too literal**—too real. For a while, **tools will lead design** as opposed to the designer leading the choice of tools. It is a process of change that we have to work through.
Rich Greenberg, designer

Design will be decentralized. The strongest move for the next generation will be into custom publishing, which can address a very narrow audience. Things will become highly technical and less aesthetic. The aesthetics and mechanics of how ideas move through electronic means are at the heart of the matter. However, graphic designers shouldn't get hung up on software or technique, since the design studio is really between their ears, not in their computer.
Tibor Kalman, designer

A better-educated, more discriminating and design-conscious consumer is demanding **better products**, better services, and a better environment. Industry and government are gradually changing to meet these demands, and this explains the consistent growth of design services. However, these services will have to become more sophisticated, and designers themselves must continue to prove to clients—and the public—that they are more than cosmeticians, that they are **problem solvers** with a unique perspective.

Colin Forbes, designer

In the future I believe there will probably be more large design firms, and as clients' needs become more international, designers will be increasingly required to blend more than one culture in their work.

Colin Forbes, designer

Social Change

Change is international. A second language will be more and more important. A background in other disciplines such as business, architecture, city planning, social sciences, history, and cultural studies will also be important. Working in different countries and different environments will become routine as will knowledge of the earth sciences. Change will be inherent as electronic information spins around the globe. The computer will be just a part of this electronic information revolution. Seeing, hearing, speaking, and touching will be connected to the computer, to digits, to satellites, making it easier to acquire knowledge and information globally.

James Miho, educator

Designers must become better equipped to deal with the client and the business world in a strategic way. They must be more than purveyors of services. They must go beyond typical design judgment and address **strategic ideas** to help the client develop new directions. Designers have a very specific role here because they are trained to be problem solvers—trained to investigate **new directions**—and by nature they do not accept the status quo. Business needs this capability, but not all designers are prepared by training or practice to work at this level. This is a window of opportunity for designers in the future.
Robert Blaich, designer

Audiences for communications are far more mixed and complex than designers have previously considered them to be. The future will be marked by our ability to be attentive to others who are not like us. Our attention to differences will make for a more humane society and a more humane design.
Sheila Levrant de Bretteville, educator

Cross-disciplinary activity is increasing in importance. This development speaks to how we teach and how we engage the opportunities for design that have clearly emerged in less traditional areas.
Deborah Sussman, designer

The promise of technology is unrealized. Today it is more about the **look** and the **process** of visual ideas and less about the means and purposes of communication. New forms of design will emerge, such as the techno-mechanical, paradesign (desktop publishing, for example), and something we might call media architecture, which brings a greater involvement with speech, sound, video, and information. As an educator I am excited by the information component, and as a pragmatist I am challenged by the expanded conceptual possibilities. Change always carries a component of the unforeseen. The conflict caused by overstatement and overreaction about what is replaced or what is retained in design education concerns all of us. I think the focus must be on ideas, meaningful issues, information, the synthesis of word and image, and a better understanding of audience and the potential uses of communication.
Doug Wadden, educator

Educational Change

Design will increase its demand for professionals who are both specialists and generalists. As the amount of information relevant to design expands, it is more difficult to be an expert in everything related to professional practice. At the same time, there is a greater need for designers to act as mediators between experts in different fields, and to be efficient in their acquisition of new knowledge. I believe designers who are **broadly educated** (in areas outside of design), but who develop focused expertise in certain areas of design practice, will be the most valuable professionals in the future. Schools that succeed will be those that commit to doing some things very well and ignoring others, while providing opportunities for students to study outside the discipline.
Meredith Davis, educator

I see enormous growth in graphic design in making things understandable, in making things usable and instructive—not in a dry way but as a rich art of understanding—an art of information.
Richard Saul Wurman, designer

There is a broader long-term evolution that will impact on **design education**. I expect that some serious visual language (graphic design) study will become part of everyone's undergraduate education. The need for this study is signaled by everyone's involvement with electronic communications, word processing, interactive media, etc. Visual language study may even creep into primary and secondary schools, possibly replacing many of the arts and crafts classes. This new **general education** component will lead to greater popular understanding of and respect for the work of professional graphic designers, just as the better you are as an amateur athlete, the more you respect the skills and dedication of the superstars.
Gordon Salchow, educator

A very strict definition of graphic design no longer works. When things are changing quickly, you've got to be a problem solver and be able to think abstractly.
Rich Greenberg, designer

This decade, as well as future eras, measures productivity in relationship to the development of new knowledge. Knowledge is the primary industrial and institutional product, and it is simultaneously the essential resource for production. In response to this shift in cultural needs, from physical object to intellectual product, **design education** must work itself out of the hand skill business and into the **thinking business.**
Dietmar Winkler, educator

The burgeoning field of educational publishing needs designers proficient in new technologies to help produce electronic books, software, videos, and multimedia products in addition to print. There are tremendous opportunities for designers to create innovative products for our country's children.

Anne Ghory-Goodman, designer

The designer, the client, and the audience are historically the three players who are involved in creating useful visual messages. Lately designers and teachers are giving much attention to the designer-client relationship as shown by topics like design project management and design presentation. A key link that has for too long gone unexplored is the one between **designers and audience**. The challenges of the future demand that teachers examine this link. Disciplines such as psychology, anthropology, and sociology can help designer and student alike get in touch with their audience. Designers, squarely face your audience! Dare I say it? Design is now a full contact sport. Direct contact with the recipients of visual communications can serve the designer as a kind of insurance for making messages more meaningful and effective.

Kevin Byrne, educator

Here are some changes that I hope are already in progress. In my view, graphic design is an **art of communication,** rather than a fine art of personal expression; this distinction needs to be made clear to students. It is critical that graphic design students be trained more fully in the history, function, and application of typography, because using computer tools requires them to be skilled typesetters as well as graphic designers. These tools are powerful. They allow type and other visual elements to be applied in very flexible and creative ways, but also to be distorted into illegibility if used without respect for the type and the message. There seems to be a real inclination to **overdesign** and overuse the computer's manipulative capabilities at the moment.
Carol Twombly, designer

Design will be even more completely integrated into other communication functions. For example, we see now that design is becoming a mainstream marketing function. These changes need to be reflected in the education of designers, who need to be better versed in other communication skills, in particular writing and presentations. I am not suggesting that visual studies be diluted—expertise in image and identity issues is important—but design needs to be located in a broader communication context.
Won Chung, designer

AIGA Chapters

The American Institute of Graphic Arts is a national nonprofit organization devoted to the advancement of excellence in graphic design. Founded in 1914, the AIGA increases public awareness of the graphic design profession through its sponsorship of exhibitions, competitions, publications, professional seminars, educational activities, and projects in the public interest.

Members of the Institute are involved in the design and production of books, magazines, and other periodicals as well as corporate, environmental, and promotional graphics. Through its thirty-five chapters nationwide, AIGA members participate in an effective, informal network of professional assistance that is a resource to the profession and to the public. AIGA chapters have programs for students. Please contact AIGA National at (800)548-1634, fax (212)755-6749, for the appropriate contact.

Anchorage, AK
Atlanta, GA
Baltimore, MD
Birmingham, AL
Boston, MA
Chicago, IL
Cincinnati, OH
Cleveland, OH
Denver, CO
Detroit, MI
Honolulu, HI
Indianapolis, IN
Jacksonville, FL
Kansas City, MO
Knoxville, TN
Los Angeles, CA
Miami, FL
Minnesota
Nebraska
New York, NY
Philadelphia, PA
Phoenix, AZ
Pittsburgh, PA
Portland, OR
Raleigh, NC
Richmond, VA
Rochester, NY
St. Louis, MO
Salt Lake City, UT
San Diego, CA
San Francisco, CA
Seattle, WA
Texas
Washington, DC
Wichita, KS

Design Organizations

Advertising Photographers of America
1725 W. North Ave.
Chicago, IL 60622
(312)342-1717

Advertising Typographers Association
5 Penn Plaza, Suite 20
New York, NY 10001

Alliance Graphique Internationale
c/o Pentagram
61 Wharf Rd.
London W2 England

American Center for Design
233 East Ontario St.
Chicago, IL 60611
(312)787-2018

American Institute of Graphic Arts
1059 Third Ave.
New York, NY 10021
(212)752-0813

American Association of Advertising Agencies
666 Third Ave.
New York, NY 10017
(212)682-2500

Art Directors Club of Los Angeles
7080 Hollywood Blvd.
Los Angeles, CA 90028
(213)465-8707

Art Directors Club of New York
250 Park Ave. S.
New York, NY 10003
(212)674-0500

Association for the Development of Electronic Publishing Techniques
360 N. Michigan
Chicago, IL 60601
(312)609-0577

Association of Professional Design Firms
955 Massachusetts Ave.
Suite 324
P.O. Box 9183
Cambridge, MA 02139
(617)884-7474

The Creative Club of Boston
155 Massachusetts Ave.
Boston, MA 02115
(617)338-6452

Dallas Society of Visual Communications
3530 Highmesa Dr.
Dallas, TX 75234
(214)241-2017

Design Management Institute
107 South St., Suite 502
Boston, MA 02111
(617)338-6380

Graphic Artists Guild
11 W. 20th St.
New York, NY 10011
(212)463-7730

Graphic Communications Association
100 Dangerfield
Alexandria, VA 22314
(703)519-8160

International Council of Graphic Design Associations
(ICOGRADA)
P.O. Box 398
London W11 4UG
England

Institute of Business Designers
341 Merchandise Mart
Chicago, IL 60654
(312)467-1950

International Association of Business Communicators
One Hallidie Plaza #600
San Francisco, CA 94102
(415)433-3400

National Composition Association
1730 Lynn St.
Arlington, VA 22209
(703)519-8165

Package Design Council
P.O. Box 1332
Pleasant Valley, NY 12569
(914)635-9153

Phoenix Society of Communicating Arts
P.O. Box 17065
Phoenix, AZ 85001
(602)389-5943

Printing Industries of America
100 Dangerfield
Alexandria, VA 22314
(703)519-8100

Society of Environmental Graphic Designers
47 Third St.
Cambridge, MA 02141
(617)577-8225

Society of Newspaper Design
The Newspaper Center
Box 17290
Dulles Intl. Airport
Washington, DC 20041
(703)620-1083

Society of Publication Designers
60 W. 42nd St.
New York, NY 10017
(212)697-1246

Type Directors Club
60 E. 42nd St.
New York, NY 10165
(212)983-6042

Typographers International Association
2233 Wisconsin Ave.
Suite 235
Washington, DC 20007
(202)965-3400

University and College Designers Association
2811 Mishakawa Ave.
South Bend, IN 46615
(219)288-8232

Design Publications

The AIGA Journal of Graphic Design
1059 Third Ave.
New York, NY 10021

Communication Arts
410 Sherman Ave.
P.O. Box 10300
Palo Alto, CA 94303

Design Issues
The MIT Press
55 Hayward St.
Cambridge, MA 02142

Design Quarterly
The MIT Press
55 Hayward St.
Cambridge, MA 02142

Emigré
48 Shattuck Square #175
Berkeley, CA 94704

Graphic Design USA
Kaye Publishing Corp.
120 E. 56th St.
New York, NY 10022

Graphis
Graphis U.S. Inc.
141 Lexington Ave.
New York, NY 10016

HOW
1507 Dana Ave.
Cincinnati, OH 45207

ID
330 W. 42nd St.
New York, NY 10036

Print
104 Fifth Ave.
New York, NY 10011

Step-By-Step Graphics
Dynamic Graphics, Inc.
6000 N. Forest Park Dr.
Peoria, IL 61614-3592

U&lc
International Typeface Corporation
866 Second Ave.
New York, NY 10017

Visible Language
Rhode Island School of Design
2 College St.
Providence, RI 02903

Directory

The following is a listing of four-year institutions that responded to AIGA questionnaires sent out in 1992 and 1993. You may want to use this listing to request catalogs, find out information about application requirements, or schedule school visits. Please remember to look at the number of faculty involved in teaching, and at the number of students enrolled in the department, so that you can identify the scope of the curriculum.

Title of institution	Université Laval	University of Alabama in Huntsville
College title	Faculté des Arts	College of Liberal Arts
School title	Ecole des Arts Visuels	
Department title		Department of Art and Art History
Program title	Communication Graphique	Graphic Design
Address	Pavillon Casult, Université Laval Quebec, Quebec, Canada GLK 7P4	Roberts Hall Dept. of Art & Art History Huntsville, AL 35899
Phone/Fax	418-656-7631/418-656-7807	205-895-6114
Coordinator's title	Director	
Type of institution	University	Public university
Degrees offered	Bachelors and Masters	BA
Total degree credits req'd	90 UG	51 UG
Total years req'd	3 UG/2 G	3 UG
Internship/Duration (in months)	Some students/1 full-time	Some students/12
Number of faculty	12 FT	1 FT
Number of students	300 UG/10 G	40 UG
Accredited		

Title of institution	University of Alaska at Anchorage	University of Montevallo
College title		Fine Arts
School title		
Department title	Art	Art Department
Program title	Graphic Emphasis	Graphic Design
Address	3911 Providence Dr. Anchorage, AK 99508	6402 Bloch Hall Montevallo, AL 35115-6402
Phone/Fax	907-786-1356/907-786-1799	205-665-6402
Coordinator's title	Chairperson	Director
Type of institution	Public university	Public university
Degrees offered	BFA, BA	BFA, BA, BS
Total degree credits req'd	121 UG	136 UG
Total years req'd	4 UG	4 UG
Internship/Duration (in months)	All students/3	All stud.(BFA), Some (BA, BS)/Varies
Number of faculty		1 FT
Number of students		25 UG
Accredited		NASAD

Title of institution	Auburn University	University of North Alabama
College title	College of Liberal Arts	
School title		Arts & Sciences
Department title	Department of Art	Art
Program title	Visual Communications	Graphic Design
Address	Biggin Hall 101 Auburn, AL 36849-5125	Seminary St. Florence, AL 35632-0001
Phone/Fax	205-844-4373	205-760-4384
Coordinator's title	Coordinator	Chairperson
Type of institution	Public university	Public university
Degrees offered	BFA, MFA	BA, BS, BFA
Total degree credits req'd	192 UG/90 G	133 UG
Total years req'd	4 UG/2 G	4 UG
Internship/Duration (in months)	Some students/4	Some students/3
Number of faculty	6 FT	3 FT
Number of students	260 UG/2 G	30 UG
Accredited	NASAD, SAC	NASAD

Title of institution	Samford University	University of South Alabama
College title	Howard College of Arts and Sciences	Arts & Sciences
School title		
Department title	Art Department	Art & Art History
Program title	Graphic Design	Graphic Design
Address	Box 2232 Birmingham, AL 35229-2232	Visual Arts Bldg. Mobile, AL 36688
Phone/Fax	205-870-2849, 205-870-2840	205-460-6335
Coordinator's title		Head
Type of institution	Private	Public university
Degrees offered	Graphic Des., Interior Des., Art Ed.	BFA
Total degree credits req'd		192 UG
Total years req'd	4 UG	4 UG
Internship/Duration (in months)	All students/3–6	Some students/5
Number of faculty	1 FT	2 FT
Number of students	50 UG	50 UG
Accredited		

Title of institution	University of Alabama	Arkansas State University
College title	Arts and Sciences	
School title	Art	Fine Arts
Department title	Art	Art Department
Program title	Graphic Design	Graphic Design
Address	Box 870270 Tuscaloosa, AL 35487-0270	Box 1920 State University, AR 72467
Phone/Fax	205-348-5967/205-348-9642	501-972-3050/501-972-3839
Coordinator's title		Chairperson
Type of institution	Public university	Public university
Degrees offered	BA, BFA	BFA, BA, BSE, MA
Total degree credits req'd	128 UG	140 UG
Total Years req'd	3 UG	4 UG/1.5 G
Internship/Duration (in months)	Some students/3	Some students/1 semester
Number of faculty	25 FT	2 FT
Number of students	80 UG	50 UG/ 2 G
Accredited	NASAD	

Title of institution	University of Alabama in Birmingham	Arkansas Tech University
College title	Academic Affairs	
School title	School of Arts & Humanities	Liberal & Fine Arts
Department title	Art	Art
Program title	Studio Art/Graphic Design	Art (Graphic Design)
Address	Dept. of Art 113 Humanities Bldg. Birmingham, AL 35294-6639	Russellville, AR 72801
Phone/Fax	205-934-4941/205-975-6639	501-968-0209/501-968-0633
Coordinator's title		
Type of institution	Public university	Public university
Degrees offered	BFA, BA w/concentration in G. design	BA in Art, Graphic Design Option
Total degree credits req'd		124 UG
Total years req'd		4 UG
Internship/Duration (in months)	Some students/3	Some students/Varies
Number of faculty	1 FT	1 FT
Number of students		42 UG
Accredited		

A–associate UG–undergraduate G–graduate FT–full-time PT–part-time

Harding University
College of Arts & Sciences

Department of Art
Graphic Design
Box 938 Station A
Searcy, AR 72149-0001
501-279-4426

Private university
BS, BFA
137 UG
4 UG
All students/9
1 FT
30 UG

University of Arkansas at Little Rock
Col. of Arts, Humanities, and Soc. Sciences

Department of Art
Graphic Design/Illustration Program
2801 S. University Ave.
Little Rock, AR 72204
501-569-3812
Coordinator
Public university
BA in Art w/emphasis in G. Des./Ill.
124 UG
4 UG
Some students/Approx. 3
2 FT
20 UG
NASAD

Arizona State University
College of Fine Arts
School of Art

Graphic Design
School of Art 102
Tempe, AZ 85287-1505
602-965-3468/602-965-8338
Coordinator
Public university
BFA
126 UG
4 UG
Some students/9
6 FT
120 UG
NCAA

Northern Arizona University
Creative & Communication Arts
School of Art and Design

Visual Communications (G. Des. & Ill.)
Box 6020
Flagstaff, AZ 86001
602-523-4431
Head
Public university
BFA
125 UG
4 UG
Some students/3+
2 FT
70+ UG

University of Arizona
College of Fine Arts

Department of Art
Graphic Design/Illustration Program
Department of Art
Tucson, AZ 85721
602-621-1251/602-621-1307
Director
Public university
BFA, MFA
125 UG/60 G
4 UG/3 G
Some students
4 FT
200 UG/6 G

Alberta College of Art

Visual Communications Department
Visual Communications
1407-14th Avenue N.W.
Calgary, Alberta, Canada T2N 4R3
403-284-7600/403-289-6682
Program Coordinator
Public college
4-year diploma

4 UG
All students
14 FT
150 UG
PAAC

Art Center College of Design

Graphic/Packaging

1700 Lida St.
Pasadena, CA 91103
818-584-5000/818-405-9104
Chairperson
Private college
BFA, MFA, BS, MS
151 UG/60 G
3–4 UG/2–3 G

34 FT
243 UG/6 G
NASAD, WAS

Academy of Art College

Graphic Design Department

540 Powell St.
San Francisco, CA 94108
415-765-4200/415-765-9057
Director
Private college
BFA, MFA
128 UG/60 G
4 UG/2–7 G
Some students/3
22 FT
322 UG/42 G
NASAD, ICD

Cal Poly State University
Liberal Arts

Dept. Art & Design

San Luis Obispo, CA 93407
805-756-1149/Same
Chairperson
Public university
BS in Applied Art & Design
198 UG
4 UG

3 FT
150 UG
NASAD

California College of Arts and Crafts
San Francisco Campus
School of Design
Graphic Design Department
Graphic Design
1700 17th St.
San Francisco, CA 94103
415-703-9500/415-621-2396
Chairperson
Private college
BFA, MFA
123 UG
2.5–3 UG
All students
2 FT
132 UG
NASAD, WAS

California Institute of the Arts

Art School
Graphic Design Department

24700 McBean Pkwy.
Valencia, CA 91355
805-255-1050/805-254-8352
Director
Private college
BFA, MFA

4 UG/2 G
No students
8 FT
30 UG/16 G
NASAD

California State Polytechnic University
College of Arts

Art Department
Option in Design
3801 W. Temple Ave.
Pomona, CA 91768
714-869-3508
Head
Public university
BA in Art (Option in Des. for Fine Arts)
186 UG
4 UG

3 FT
233 UG

California State University, Los Angeles

School of Arts & Letters
Art Department
BA/MA/MFA
5151 State University Dr.
Los Angeles, CA 90032
213-343-4010/213-343-4045
Chairperson
Public university
BA, MA, MFA
186 UG/ 45–90 G
4 UG/1–2 G
Some students/6
3 FT
216 UG/18 G
NASAD, WAS

California State University, Stanislaus
Arts, Letters and Sciences

Art Department
Fine Art Printmaking
801 W. Monte Vista Avenue
Turlock, CA 95380

Public university

California State Univ., Dominguez Hills

Humanities & Fine Arts
Art Department
Bachelor of Arts in Art Option Design
1000 E. Victoria Street
Carson, CA 90747

Public university
BA
124 UG
4 UG
All students
4 FT
50 UG
NASAD

California State University, Fullerton

Art Department
Design

800 N. State College Blvd.
Fullerton, CA 92634
714-773-3471
Head
Public university
BA, BFA, MA, MFA
132 UG/60 G
5 UG/ 2 G
Some Students/4.5
5 FT
30 UG/15 G
NASAD, WASC

Humboldt State University
College of Creative Arts & Humanities

Art Department
BA (studio concentration in G. Design)

Arcata, CA 95521
707-826-3624/707-826-5555
Chairperson
Public university
BA
124 UG
4 UG
Some students
2 FT
50 UG
NASAD

Otis/Parsons School of Art and Design

Communication Design and Illustration

2401 Wilshire Boulevard
Los Angeles, CA 90057
213-251-0514/213-480-0059
Chairperson
Private college
BFA
134 UG
4UG
Some students/6
2 FT
42 PT
NASAD, WAS

Title of institution	**San Jose State University**	**Metropolitan State College of Denver**
College title	College of Humanities and the Arts	
School title		School of Arts and Letters
Department title	Department of Art and Design	Art Department
Program title	Graphic Design	Advertising Design
Address	One Washington Square San Jose, CA 95192-0089	Campus Box 59, PO Box 173362 Denver, CO 80217-3362
Phone/Fax	408-924-4321/408-924-4326	303-556-3090/303-556-3091
Coordinator's title	Area Coordinator	Coordinator
Type of institution	Public university	Public college
Degrees offered	BS in Graphic Design	BFA
Total degree credits req'd	132 UG/30 G	66 UG
Total years req'd	4–5 UG/2–3 G	4 UG
Internship/Duration (in months)	Some students/Open	Some students
Number of faculty	3 FT	2 FT
Number of students	110 UG/3 G	30 UG
Accredited	NASAD	

Title of institution	**Scripps College**	**Rocky Mountain College of Art & Design**
College title		
School title		
Department title	Art Department	
Program title	Electronic Imaging	Advertising and Graphic Design
Address	1030 Columbia Claremont, CA 91711	6875 East Evans Avenue Denver, CO 80224
Phone/Fax	714-621-8000/714-621-8323	303-753-6046/303-759-4970
Coordinator's title		Chairperson
Type of institution	Private college	Private college
Degrees offered	BA	BA
Total degree credits req'd		128 UG
Total years req'd	2–3 UG	4 UG
Internship/Duration (in months)		All students/90 hrs.
Number of faculty	1 FT	5 FT
Number of students		87 UG
Accredited	WASC	CCA

Title of institution	**University of San Francisco**	**University of Southern Colorado**
College title	BFA College of Art & Science	College of Humanities and Social Sciences
School title		
Department title	Graphic Design	Art Department
Program title	Cooperative Bachelor of Fine Arts Prog.	Graphic Design
Address	540 Powell Street San Francisco, CA 94108	2200 Benforte Pueblo, CO 81001-4901
Phone/Fax	415-765-4227	719-549-2835
Coordinator's title	Director	Professor
Type of institution	Private university	University
Degrees offered	BA of Fine Arts	BA, BS
Total degree credits req'd	128 UG	128 UG
Total years req'd	4–5 UG	4 UG
Internship/Duration (in months)	Some students/1 semester	Some students/3
Number of faculty	1 FT	1 FT
Number of students	25 UG	20 UG
Accredited	NASAD, CCA	NASAD

Title of institution	**University of the Pacific**	**Central Connecticut State University**
College title	College of the Pacific	
School title		
Department title	Department of Art	Art
Program title	Graphic Design	Graphic Design
Address	 Stockton, CA 95211	1615 Stanley St., Samuel S.T. Chen Art Ctr. New Britain, CT 06050
Phone/Fax	209-946-2241	203-827-7963/203-827-7046
Coordinator's title	Head	Head
Type of institution	Private university	Public university
Degrees offered	BFA	BA in Art/Graphic Design
Total degree credits req'd	136 UG	122 UG
Total years req'd	4 UG	4 UG
Internship/Duration (in months)	Some students/1 semester	Some students/4
Number of faculty	2 FT	3 FT
Number of students	30 UG	75 UG
Accredited	NASAD	NEASC

Title of institution	**Woodbury University**	**Connecticut College**
College title		
School title		
Department title	Department of Graphic Design	Department of Art
Program title		
Address	7500 Glenoaks Blvd. Burbank, CA 91510	270 Mohegan Avenue New London, CT 06320
Phone/Fax	818-767-0888/818-504-9320	203-439-2700 (Fax)
Coordinator's title	Chairperson	Chairman
Type of institution	Private university	Private college
Degrees offered	BS in Graphic Design, MBA in Business	BA in Studio Art
Total degree credits req'd	188 UG	128 UG
Total years req'd	4 UG	4 UG
Internship/Duration (in months)	Some students/3	
Number of faculty	4 FT	1 FT
Number of students	70 UG	15 UG
Accredited		NEASC

Title of institution	**Colorado State University**	**Univ. of Hartford**
College title	Arts, Humanities, & Social Sciences	Hartford Art School
School title		
Department title	Department of Art	
Program title	Graphic Design	Graphic Design
Address	CSU Art Dept. Fort Collins, CO 80523	200 Bloomfield Ave. West Hartford, CT 06117
Phone/Fax	303-491-6774/303-491-0505	203-768-4393
Coordinator's title		
Type of institution	Public university	Private university
Degrees offered	BFA	BFA
Total degree credits req'd	128 UG	121 UG
Total years req'd	4 UG	3 UG
Internship/Duration (in months)	All students/4 semesters	Some students/6
Number of faculty	3.5 FT	3 FT
Number of students	130 UG	30 UG
Accredited		NASAD, NEA

A–associate UG–undergraduate G–graduate FT–full-time PT–part-time

Paier College of Art Inc.

Division of Design
Graphic Design
6 Prospect Ct.
Hamden, CT 06517-4025
203-777-7319
Director
Private college
BFA
130 UG
4 UG

4.5 FT
50 UG
CBR

University of Connecticut

School of Fine Arts
Art
Graphic Design
875 Conventry Rd.
Storrs, CT 06269
203-486-3930

Public university
BFA, MFA
120 UG/60 G
4 UG/2 G
All students/112 hrs.
4 FT
230 UG
NASAD

Tunxis Community College

Social Science
Applied Arts in Graphic Design
Routes 6 & 177
Farmington, CT 06032
203-677-7701

Public college

2 UG
Some students/4
1 FT
30 UG

Yale University

School of Art
Department of Graphic Design

Box 2004 Yale Station
New Haven, CT 06520-2004
203-432-2622/203-432-7158
Director
Private university
MFA, BA
60 G
3 UG/2–3 G
No students
2 FT
3 UG/38 G
NASAD

University of Alberta

Department of Art and Design
Visual Communication Design
Fine Arts Bldg. 3-86
Edmonton, Alberta, Canada T6G 2C9
403-492-5789
Coordinator
Public university
BA, BFA, Bachelor of Design
123 UG
4 UG/2 G
Some students
2 FT
120 UG/4 G

York University
Faculty of Fine Arts

Department of Visual Arts
Visual Communication Design
4700 Keele St., North York
Toronto, Ontario, Canada M3J 1P3
416-736-5187/416-736-5447
Area Representative
Public university
BA, BFA, MFA
20 UG/5 G
4 UG/2.5 G
Some students/Varies
3 FT
120 UG/4 G

Corcoran School of Art

Graphic Design
Fine Art
500 17th St. NW
Washington, DC 20006-4899
202-628-9484/202-628-3186
Chairperson
Private
BFA
126 UG
3 UG
All students/3.5
2.5 FT
26 UG
NASAD, MAS (Mid Atlantic States)

Mount Vernon College
Arts and Humanities
Studio Arts/Graphic Design

2100 Foxhall Rd. NW
Washington, DC 20007
202-625-4648
Chairperson
Private college
Interior Design, Studio Arts, Graphics

4 UG
6
1 FT

American University
College of Arts and Sciences

Department of Art
Design Program
Watkins Bldg., 400 Mass. Ave. NW
Washington, DC 20016
202-885-1671
Head
Private university
BA
54 UG
4 UG
Some students/3–6
4 FT
2 UG/50 G

Trinity College

Arts and Humanities
Art Program
125 Michigan Ave. NE
Washington, DC 20017
202-939-5178/202-939-5134
Chairperson
Private college
BA
128 UG
4 UG
No students
.5 FT
4 UG

Flagler College

Visual Art
Commercial Art
74 King Street
St. Augustine, FL 30284
904-829-6481
Chairperson
Public university
BA
120 UG
4 UG
Some students/3
4 FT
80 UG
SAC

Florida State University

School of Visual Arts and Dance
Fine Arts

220 FAB R-133
Tallahassee, FL 32306-2037
904-644-6474/904-644-8977
Chairperson
Public university
BA, BS (120 credits), BFA (132 credits)
120 UG/60 G
2 UG
All students/3–9 credit
2 FT
25 UG/3–5 G
NASAD , SAC

Jacksonville University
College of Fine Arts

Department of Art
Visual Comm., Computer Art and Des.
2800 University Blvd. N.
Jacksonville, FL 32211
904-744-3950
Head
Private university
BFA, BA, BS
128 UG
4 UG
All students/6 credit
1 FT
80 UG
SACS

Ringling School of Art & Design

Graphic Design Department

2700 North Tamiami Trail
Sarasota, FL 34234-5895
813-351-4614/813-351-7517
Head
Private college
BFA

3 UG
Some students/9
5 FT
95 UG
NASAD, SAC

University of Central Florida

Department of Art
Graphic Design
Box 25000
Orlando, FL 32816
407-823-2676/407-823-5156

Public university
BA, BFA
120 UG
4 UG
All students (in Graphic Design)/4
1 FT
70+ UG/4 G

University of Florida
College of Fine Arts

Department of Art
Graphic Design
Department of Art & Graphic Design
Gainesville, FL 32611-2032
904-392-8670
Coordinator
Public university
BD, MFA
130 UG
2 UG/3 G
No students
3 FT
30 UG/2 G
SACS

University of Miami
College of Arts and Sciences

Department of Art and Art History
Graphic Design and Illustration
1300 Campo Sano Drive
Coral Gables, FL 33124
305-284-2543
Coordinator
Public university
BA, BFA, MFA
120 UG
4 UG/2 G

2 FT
75 UG/2 G

University of North Florida
Arts and Sciences

Communications and Visual Arts
Graphic Design
4567 St. Johns Bluff Rd. S.
Jacksonville, FL 32216-6699
904-646-2650/904-646-2703
Head
Public university
BA, BFA
120 UG
2 UG
Some students/4
3 FT
75 UG
SACS

A–associate UG–undergraduate G–graduate FT–full-time PT–part-time

Title of institution	**Atlanta College of Art**	**Graceland College**
College title		
School title		
Department title	Communication Design Department	Art Department
Program title	Advertising Design, Graphic Design, Ill.	Art-Commercial Design
Address	1280 Peachtree St. NE Atlanta, GA 30309	700 College Ave. Lamoni, IA 50140
Phone/Fax	404-898-1164/404-898-9577	515-784-5000/515-784-5480
Coordinator's title	Head	Head
Type of institution	Private college	Private college
Degrees offered	BFA	Comm. Art, Studio Art, Publication Design
Total degree credits req'd	129 UG	128 UG
Total years req'd	3 UG	4 UG
Internship/Duration (in months)	Some students	All students/1–3
Number of faculty	2 FT	3 FT
Number of students	90 UG	15 UG
Accredited	NASAD, SAC	NASAD

Title of institution	**Georgia State University**	**Iowa State University**
College title	College of Arts and Sciences	College of Design
School title	School of Art and Design	
Department title	Graphic Design	Department of Art & Design
Program title		Graphic Design
Address	University Plaza Atlanta, GA 30303-3083	158 College of Design Ames, IA 50011-3092
Phone/Fax	404-651-2257/404-651-2013	515-294-6724/515-294-9755
Coordinator's title	Coordinator	Coordinator
Type of institution	Public university	Public university
Degrees offered	BFA, BA, MFA, MA	BFA, MFA, MA
Total degree credits req'd	210 UG	127 UG/60 G
Total years req'd	4–5 UG	4 UG/2–3 G
Internship/Duration (in months)	All students/3-6	Some students/2–4
Number of faculty	3 FT	6 FT
Number of students	30 UG	80 UG/8–10 G
Accredited	NASAD	

Title of institution	**Savannah College of Art and Design**	**Mount Mercy College**
College title		
School title		
Department title	Graphic Design Department	Art Department
Program title		Graphic Design Concentration
Address	201 W. Charlton St., Box 3146 Savannah, GA 31402-3146	1330 Elmhurst Dr. NE Cedar Rapids, IA 52402-4798
Phone/Fax	912-238-2487/912-238-2436	319-363-8213/319-363-5270
Coordinator's title	Chairman	Chairman
Type of institution	Private college	Private college
Degrees offered	BFA, MFA	BA
Total degree credits req'd	180 hrs. UG/90 hrs. G	123 UG
Total years req'd	4UG/2G	4 UG
Internship/Duration (in months)	Some students/2.5	Some students/2
Number of faculty	8 FT	
Number of students	550 UG/50 G	4 UG
Accredited	SACS	

Title of institution	**University of Georgia**	**St. Ambrose University**
College title	Franklin College of Arts & Sciences	College of Arts & Sciences
School title	School of Art	
Department title		Art
Program title	Program of Graphic Design	Graphic Design
Address	Jackson St. Athens, GA 30602	518 W. Locust St. Davenport, IA 52803
Phone/Fax	404-542-1567	319-383-8800
Coordinator's title	Chairman	Chairperson
Type of institution	Public university	Private university
Degrees offered	BFA	BA
Total degree credits req'd	210 UG	120 UG
Total years req'd	2.5 UG	4 UG
Internship/Duration (in months)	All students/3	Some students/1 semester
Number of faculty	6 FT	
Number of students	60 UG	16–20 UG
Accredited	NASAD	

Title of institution	**Valdosta State College**	**University of Northern Iowa**
College title		College of Humanities & Fine Arts
School title	School of the Arts	
Department title	Department of Art	Department of Art
Program title	BA (Fine Arts, Arts, Fine Arts in Art Ed.)	Graphic Design
Address	Fine Arts Bldg. Valdosta, GA 31698	Kamerick Art Bldg. Cedar Falls, IA 50614-0362
Phone/Fax	912-333-5834	319-273-2077
Coordinator's title	Professor	
Type of institution	Public college	Public university
Degrees offered	BFA, BFA in Art Ed., BA with major in art	BA, BFA, MA
Total degree credits req'd	205 UG	124 UG/30 G
Total years req'd	4 UG	2 UG/2 G
Internship/Duration (in months)		Some students/4–8
Number of faculty	1.5 FT	2 FT
Number of students		75 UG/5 G
Accredited	SACS	NASAD

Title of institution	**University of Hawaii-Manoa**	**Boise State University**
College title	College of Arts and Sciences	Arts & Sciences
School title		
Department title	Department of Art	Art
Program title	Graphic Design	Graphic Design
Address	2535 The Mall Honolulu, HI 96822	1910 University Dr. Boise, ID 83725
Phone/Fax	808-956-8251	208-385-1230
Coordinator's title	Program Chair	Chairperson
Type of institution	Public university	Public university
Degrees offered	BA, BFA, MFA	BA, BFA
Total degree credits req'd	133 UG/60 G	128 UG
Total years req'd	4.5 UG/2.5 G	4 UG
Internship/Duration (in months)	Some students/5–12	Some students/6
Number of faculty	3 FT	4 FT
Number of students	135 UG	150 UG
Accredited		

A–associate UG–undergraduate G–graduate FT–full time PT–part time

University of Idaho
Art & Architecture

Art
BFA of Art (Graphic Design)

Moscow, ID 83843
208-885-6851/208-885-5555
Chairperson
Public university
BFA Art, BFA Photo., BA Art, BS Art Ed.
128 UG/60 G
4 UG/3 G
All students/Varies
1 FT
30–40 UG/2 G

Bradley University
College of Communications and Fine Art

Division of Art
Graphic Des. and Ill.
Hewser Art Center
Peproa, IL 61625
309-677-3332
Head
Private university
BA, BS, BFA, MA, MFA
124 UG/60 G
3 UG
Some students/Varies
3 FT
125 UG
NASAD

Columbia College Chicago

Art and Design
Graphic Design
600 South Michigan
Chicago, IL 60605
312-663-1600
Chairperson
Private college
BA
124 UG
4 UG
Some students/4
6 FT
150 UG
North Central

Illinois Institute of Technology
Institute of Design

Communication Design
10 West 35th Street
Chicago, IL 60616-3793
312-567-3250/312-567-8905

Public university
BS, MS, MDES, PHD
131 UG/32 G
4 UG

3 FT
15 UG/10 G

Illinois State University
College of Fine Arts

Department of Art
Graphic Design
5620 Department of Art
Normal, IL 61761
309-438-5621/309-438-8318
Coordinator
Public university
BA, BS, BFA, MA, MS, MFA
120 UG/60 G
2.5 UG/2 G
Some students/3
4 FT
170 UG
NASAD

Illinois State University
Fine Arts

Art
Graphic Design
Center for the Visual Arts
Normal, IL 61761
309-438-5621
Chairman
Public university
BA, BS, BFA
120 UG
4 UG
Some students/3–6
4 FT
300 UG
NASAD

Illinois Wesleyan University

School of Art

Studio Art—Graphic Design
Box 2900
Bloomington, IL 61702-2900
309-556-3077
Director
Private university
BA, BFA
32 UG
4 UG
Some students/3–7
4 FT
40 UG

Judson College

Art Department
Visual Communication
1151 N. State St.
Elgin, IL 60123
708-695-2500
Chairperson
Private college
BA
123 UG
4 UG
Some students/4–16
2 FT
20 UG
CACS

Northern Illinois University
Col. of Visual & Performing Arts
School of Art

Design–Visual Communication
Jack Arends Hall
Dekalb, IL 60115–2883
815-753-1473
Chairperson
Public university
BFA, MA, MFA
124 UG/60 G
4 UG/2 G
Some students/Optional
7 FT
325 UG/8 G
NASAD

Ray College of Design

Communications Design
Graphic Design / Advertising Design
401 N. Wabash Ave.
Chicago, IL 60611
312-280-3500/312-280-3528

Private college
BA of Arts/Advertising Design
120 UG

All students/Varies
10 FT
150 UG
CCA/ NATTS

Saint Xavier University

Art Dept.
Graphic Design
3700 W. 103rd St.
Chicago, IL 60655
312-298-3080/312-779-9061
Coordinator
Private university
BA

4 UG
Some students/3–4
1.5 FT

Southern Illinois University at Carbondale
College of Communications and Fine Arts
School of Art & Design
Design
Visual Communication
School of Art & Design/Allyn Bldg.
Carbondale, IL 62901
618-453-4315/618-453-3000

Public university
BA
120 UG
3 UG
Some students/4
4 FT
136 UG
NASAD

School of the Art Institute of Chicago

Visual Communication

375 Wabash
Chicago, IL 60613
312-889-5190/263-0141

Private college
BFA, MFA
130 UG/60 G
3.5 UG
All students/Optional
4 FT
25–30 UG/15 G
NASAD

University of Illinois
College of Fine & Applied Arts
School of Art and Design
Graphic Design

408 E. Peabody Dr.
Champaign, IL 61820
217-333-0855/217-244-7688
Chairperson
Public university
BFA, MFA
122 UG/16 G
4 UG/2 G

7 FT
135 UG/14 G
NASAD

University of Illinois at Chicago
College of Art, Arch., & Urban Planning
School of Art and Design
Graphic Design Department

UIC School of Art & Design
106 Jefferson Hall, Chicago, IL 60680
312-996-3337/312-996-5378
Head
Public university
BFA, MFA
135 UG/64 G
4 UG/2 G
Some students/1 semester
8 FT
130 UG/8 G
NASAD

Western Illinois University
College of Fine Arts

Art Department
Advertising Design
Garwood Hall 25
Malomb, IL 61455
309-298-1586
Director
Public university
BA
120 UG
3 UG

3 FT
85 UG
NASAD

Goshen College

Department of Art

1700 South Main
Goshen, IN 46526
219-535-7400/219-535-7660

Private college
BA
120 UG
4 UG
Some students/1

15 UG

Anderson University

School of Music and Art
Art Department
Graphic Design
1100 E. 5th Street
Anderson, IN 46012
317-641-4323
Director
Private college
BA
124 UG
4 UG
All students/4
1 FT
30 UG

A–associate UG–undergraduate G–graduate FT–full time PT–part time

Title of institution	**Ball State University**	**Kansas State University**
College title	College of Fine Arts	Arts and Sciences
School title		
Department title	Department of Art	Art Department
Program title	Graphic Design	Graphic Design
Address	Department of Art Muncie, IN 47306	Art Bldg. Manhattan, KS 66506
Phone/Fax	317-285-5838	913-532-6605/913-842-9137
Coordinator's title		Head
Type of institution	Public university	Public university
Degrees offered	BFA	BFA, BA, MFA
Total degree credits req'd	126 UG	120 UG/60 G
Total years req'd	4 UG	4 UG/2–3 G
Internship/Duration (in months)	Some students/3	Some students/1–3 semesters
Number of faculty	3 FT	4 FT
Number of students	120 UG	180 UG/7 G
Accredited	NASAD	

Title of institution	**Grace College**	**Fort Hays State University**
College title		School of Arts & Sciences
School title		
Department title	Art Department	Department of Art
Program title		BFA in Graphic Design Program
Address	200 Seminary Dr. Winona Lake, IN 46590	600 Park St. Hays, KS 67601
Phone/Fax	219-372-5100	913-628-4247/913-628-4096
Coordinator's title	Chairman	Associate
Type of institution	Private college	Public university
Degrees offered	BS	BFA. MFA, MA
Total degree credits req'd	124 UG	154 UG/60 G
Total years req'd	3 UG	4.5 UG/3 G
Internship/Duration (in months)	Some students/4	All students/5
Number of faculty	2 FT	2 FT
Number of students	41 UG	56 UG/2 G
Accredited		

Title of institution	**Indiana U.—Purdue U. at Indianapolis**	**University of Kansas**
College title		
School title	Herron School of Art	School of Fine Arts
Department title	Department of Visual Communication	Design Department
Program title		Visual Communication
Address	1701 N. Pennsylvania St. Indianapolis, IN 46202	300 Art & Design Bldg. Lawrence, KS 66054-2266
Phone/Fax	317-274-5555	913-864-4401/913-864-5387
Coordinator's title	Chairperson	Chairperson
Type of institution	Public university	Public university
Degrees offered	BFA	BFA, MFA
Total degree credits req'd		124 UG/60 G
Total years req'd	4 UG	4 UG
Internship/Duration (in months)	Some students/4	Some students/3–6
Number of faculty	7 FT	5 FT
Number of students	100 UG	140 UG
Accredited	NASAD, NCA	NASAD

Title of institution	**Indiana U.—Purdue U. at Fort Wayne**	**Brescia College**
College title		
School title	School of Fine Arts & Performing Arts	
Department title	Department of Fine Arts	Art
Program title	Graphic Design	Graphic Design Major
Address	2101 Coliseum Blvd. E. Fort Wayne, IN 46805	717 Frederica Street Owensboro, KY 42301
Phone/Fax	219-484-6705	502-685-3131/502-686-4266
Coordinator's title	Chairperson	Head
Type of institution	Public university	Private college
Degrees offered	BFA, AS	BA
Total degree credits req'd	124 UG	56 UG
Total years req'd	4 UG	4 UG
Internship/Duration (in months)		Some students/4
Number of faculty	3 FT	1 FT
Number of students	145 UG	25 UG
Accredited		

Title of institution	**Purdue University**	**Eastern Kentucky University**
College title		Arts and Humanities
School title	Liberal Arts	
Department title	Visual and Performing Arts	Department of Art
Program title	Visual Communication Design	Graphic Design/Illustration
Address	1352 CA-1 Building West Lafayette, IN 47907-1352	309 Campbell Bldg. Richmond, KY 40475
Phone/Fax	317-494-3058/317-496-1198	606-622-1629
Coordinator's title	Area Head	Chairman
Type of institution	Public university	Public university
Degrees offered	BA, MA, PhD (Art Education)	BFA
Total degree credits req'd	126 UG/33 G	128 UG
Total years req'd	4 UG/2 G	4 UG
Internship/Duration (in months)	Some students/Open	Some students/Varies
Number of faculty	4 FT	1 FT
Number of students	140 UG/6 G	25 UG
Accredited	NASAD, NEA	

Title of institution	**University of Notre Dame**	**Murray State University**
College title	Arts and Letters	College of Fine Arts and Communication
School title		
Department title	Dept. of Art, Art History, and Design	Department of Art
Program title	Design	Graphic Design
Address	Dept. of Art, Art History, and Design Notre Dame, IN 46556-56389	Art Department/ Price Doyle Bldg. Murray, KY 42071
Phone/Fax	219-239-7452/219-239-8209	502-762-3784/502-762-6335
Coordinator's title	Director	
Type of institution	Private university	Public university
Degrees offered	BA, BFA, MA, MFA	BA, BS, BFA, MA
Total degree credits req'd	120 UG/60 G	
Total years req'd	4 UG/3 G	4 UG/2 G
Internship/Duration (in months)	No students	Some students/3
Number of faculty		14 FT
Number of students	65 UG/2 G	
Accredited		NADAD

A–associate UG–undergraduate G–graduate FT–full-time PT–part-time

Northern Kentucky University
Arts and Sciences

Department of Art
Graphic Design
FAC 224, NKU, Nunn Dr.
Highland Heights, KY 41099
606-572-5421/606-572-5566

Public University
BA, BFA
128 UG
4–5 UG
Some students
3 FT
106 UG

University of Kentucky
College of Fine Arts

Department of Art
Studio Art (emphasis in Graphic Design)
Room 207 Fine Arts
Lexington, KY 40506-0022
606-257-2727/606-257-3042
Head
Public university
BA, BFA
120 UG
1 UG
All students/6–12

30–35 UG

Western Kentucky University
Potter C. of Arts, Human. & Soc. Sciences

Department of Art

Dept. of Art, Ivan Wilson Fine Arts Ctr., W
Bowling Green, KY 42101
502-745-3944
Head
Public university
BA, BFA, MAE
120 UG/36 G
4 UG/1 G
Some students
3 FT
125 UG
NASAD, NCA

Louisiana State University
College of Design
School of Art
Graphic Design Area
Graphic Design
123 Design Center, LSU
Baton Rouge, LA 70803
504-388-5411
Area Coordinator
Public university
BFA
132 UG
4 UG
Some students/6
5 FT
160 UG
NASAD

Louisiana Tech University
Arts and Sciences
Art and Architecture
Graphic Design

Box 3175 T.S.
Ruston, LA 71270
318-257-3909
Head
Public university
BFA, MFA
140 UG/60 G
4 UG/2 G
Some students/3
2 FT
120 UG/5 G
NASAD

McNeese State University
Liberal Arts

Visual Arts
Advertising Design
Box 92295
Lake Charles, LA 70609
318-475-5060

Public university
BA Visual Art/Fashion Design
130 UG
4 UG
All students/3
1 FT
70 UG

Northeast Louisiana University
Liberal Arts

Department of Art
Graphic Design
NLU-Art Dept.
Monroe, LA 71209-0310
318-342-1375 (Fax)

Public university
BFA
129 UG
3 UG
No students
1 FT
50 UG
SACS

University of New Orleans
Liberal Arts

Fine Arts
Graphic Design
Lakefront
New Orleans, LA 70148
504-286-7367
Graphic Design Coordinator
Public university
BA, MFA
128 UG/60 G
3 UG/3 G
Some students/4–8
1 FT

NASAD

University of Southwestern Louisiana

School of Art and Architecture
Visual Arts Department
Advertising Design
USL Box 43368
Lafayette, LA 70504
318-231-5327/318-231-5907
Professor
Public university
BFA
130 UG
2 UG

1 FT
20 UG

Montserrat College of Art

Graphic Design Department
Graphic Design
Box 26 Dunham Rd.
Beverly, MA 01915
508-922-8222
Chairman
Private college
Diploma, BFA
120 UG
4 UG
Some students/3
2 FT
35 UG
NEASC

Butera School of Art

Commercial Art/Graphic Design

111 Beacon St.
Boston, MA 02116
617-536-4623
Director
Private college
Diploma only

3 UG
Some students/4–8

NATTS

Clark University

Department of Visual & Performing Arts
Graphic Des. Concentration/Studio Art Major
950 Main St.
Worcester, MA 01610
508-793-7113

Private university
BA
32 UG
4 UG
Some students/3–6
1 FT

Fitchburg State College

Communications/Media
Graphic Design
160 Pearl Street
Fitchburg, MA 01420
508-345-2151/508-343-8603
Head
Public college
BS in Communications/Media
120 UG
4 UG
All students/3.5
2 FT
85 UG

Massachusetts College of Art

Communication Design
Graphic Design
621 Huntington Ave.
Boston, MA 02115
617-232-1555 , x346
Chairperson
Public college
BFA, MFA
132 UG/60 G
4 UG/2 G
All students
7 FT
145 UG/12 G
NASAD, NEA

Anna Maria College for Men & Women

Department of Art
Studio Art
Moll Art Center
Paxton, MA 01612
508-757-4586, x261
Chairperson
Private college
BA
120 UG
4 UG
All students/4
1 FT
5 UG
NEAA

Salem State College

Art Department
Graphic Design
352 Lafayette St.
Salem, MA 01970
508-741-6222
Chairperson
Public college
BA
127 UG
4 UG
Some students/3–6
3 FT
125 UG
NASAD

Art Institute of Boston

Graphic Design Department

700 Beacon St.
Boston, MA 02215
617-262-1223
Chairperson
Private college
BFA
124 UG
4 UG
All students/4
2 FT
65 UG
NASAD

New England School of Art & Design

Graphic Design Department
Graphic Design
28 Newbury St.
Boston, MA 02116
617-536-0383
Chairman
Private college
BFA (in conjunction with Suffolk U.)
128 UG
3 UG
Some students/8
5 FT
34 UG
NATTS, FID

A–associate UG–undergraduate G–graduate FT–full-time PT–part-time

Title of institution	**University of Massachusetts at Lowell**	**Portland School of Art**
College title	Fine Arts	
School title		
Department title	Art	Graphic Design
Program title		
Address	Durgin Hall, Rm. 430 Lowell, MA 01854	97 Spring St. Portland, ME 04101
Phone/Fax	508-934-3850	207-775-3052/207-772-5069
Coordinator's title	Chairperson	Chairman
Type of institution	Public university	Private college
Degrees offered	BA, BFA	BFA
Total degree credits req'd	120 UG	134 UG
Total years req'd		4 UG
Internship/Duration (in months)	Some Students/3–4	Some students/3
Number of faculty	2 FT	3 FT
Number of students	15 UG	20 UG
Accredited	NASAD	NASAD, NEA

Title of institution	**Westfield State College**	**Adrian College**
College title		
School title		
Department title	Art Department	Art & Design
Program title	Concentration in Graphic Design	Bachelor of Arts, Bachelor of Fine Arts
Address	Western Ave. Westfield, MA 01086	110 S. Madison Adrian, MI 49221
Phone/Fax	413-568-3311/413-562-3613	517-265-5161/517-264-3331
Coordinator's title	Chairman	Chairperson
Type of institution	Public college	Private college
Degrees offered	BA	BA, BFA
Total degree credits req'd	120 UG	36/72 UG
Total years req'd	4 UG	4 UG
Internship/Duration (in months)	Some students/3–4	Some students
Number of faculty	3 FT	.5
Number of students	45 UG	
Accredited		NCAA

Title of institution	**Mount St. Mary's College**	**Alma College**
College title		
School title		
Department title	Graphic Arts	Department of Art & Design
Program title		Visual Communication
Address	Emmitsburg, MD 21727	614 W. Superior Alma, MI 48801
Phone/Fax	301-447-5774	517-463-7111/517-463-7277
Coordinator's title		Chairperson
Type of institution	Private college	Private college
Degrees offered	BA, MA in Business & Theology	BA, BFA
Total degree credits req'd		72 UG
Total years req'd	4 UG	4 UG
Internship/Duration (in months)	Some students/1 semester	All students/4–12
Number of faculty	2 FT	1 FT
Number of students	12 UG	15-20 UG
Accredited		NCAA

144

Title of institution	**Towson State University**	**Central Michigan University**
College title	Fine Arts & Communication	Arts and Sciences
School title	Fine Arts	
Department title	Art	Art
Program title	Visual Communication Design	Graphic Design
Address	York Road Towson, MD 21204	149 Wightman Mt. Pleasant, MI 48859
Phone/Fax	410-830-2808	517-774-3025
Coordinator's title	Chairman	Director
Type of institution	Public university	Public university
Degrees offered	BA, MFA	BBA, BFA, MA, MFA
Total degree credits req'd	60 UG/36 G	124 UG/70 G
Total years req'd	4 UG	
Internship/Duration (in months)	All students/100 hours	Some students/3
Number of faculty	5 FT	1 FT
Number of students	75 UG/5 G	85 UG/3 G
Accredited		NASAD

Title of institution	**Frostburg State University**	**Cranbrook Academy of Art**
College title		
School title	School of Arts & Humanities	
Department title	Visual Arts	Design
Program title	Graphic Design	Graphic Design
Address	Rm. 205B Fine Arts Bldg. Frostburg, MD 21532	Box 801, 500 Lone Pine Rd. Bloomfield Hills, MI 48303-0801
Phone/Fax	301-689-4698/301-689-4737	313-645-3300/313-646-0046
Coordinator's title	Chairman	Chairperson
Type of institution	Public university	Private
Degrees offered	BA, BS, BFA	MFA
Total degree credits req'd	108 UG	60 G
Total years req'd	2 UG	2 G
Internship/Duration (in months)	All Students/3	
Number of faculty	8.6 FT	1 FT
Number of students		12 G
Accredited		NASAD

Title of institution	**Maryland Institute**	**Eastern Michigan University**
College title	College of Art	College of Arts and Sciences
School title		
Department title	Visual Communication	Department of Art
Program title	Graphic Design/Illustration	Visual Communications
Address	1300 Mt. Royal Ave. Baltimore, MD 21217	114 Ford Hall Ypsilanti, MI 48197
Phone/Fax	410-225-2239/410-669-9206	313-487-3388/313-481-1095, x43
Coordinator's title	Chairperson	Director
Type of institution	Private college	Public university
Degrees offered	BFA	BA, BFA, MA, MFA
Total degree credits req'd	132 UG	124 UG/30–60 G
Total years req'd	3 UG	4–5 UG/1–2 G
Internship/Duration (in months)	All students/4	Some students/Varies
Number of faculty	2 FT	4 FT
Number of students	75 UG	120 UG/10 G
Accredited	NASAD	

A–associate UG–undergraduate G–graduate FT–full-time PT–part-time

Grand Valley State University
Arts and Humanities

Art & Design
Graphic Design
Calder Fine Arts Bldg.
Allendale, MI 49401
616-895-3486/616-895-3106
Chairperson
Public university
BS, BA, BFA
122 UG
4 UG
All students/3
3 FT
60 UG
NASAD

Kendall College of Art and Design

Design Studios
Visual Communications
111 North Division
Grand Rapids, MI 49503
616-451-2787/616-451-9867
Chairman
Private college
BFA
120 UG
4 UG
All students/15-wk. semester
5 FT
100 UG
NASAD

Marygrove College

Art Department

8425 West Nichols
Detroit, MI 48221
313-884-1038/313-864-6670
Head
Private college
BA, BFA
128 UG
4–5 UG
All students/3–6
2 FT
5 UG

Michigan State University
College of Arts and Letters

Department of Art
Design
113 Kresge Art Center
East Lansing, MI 48824-1119
517-355-7611/517-355-6577
Coordinator
Public university
BA, BFA, MFA
120 UG/60 G
4 UG/2 G
Some students/Varies
4 FT
200 UG/5 G

Northern Michigan University
Arts and Sciences

Art & Design
Graphic Communications

Marquette, MI 49855
906-227-1483/906-227-2276
Professor
Public university
BFA, BA, BS, MA
131 UG/32 G
4 UG/2 G
All students/3
2 FT
55 UG/1 G
NASAD

Siena Heights College

Art Division
Graphics
1247 E. Siena Heights Dr.
Adrian, MI 49221
517-263-0731/517-265-3380
Chairperson
Private college
BA, AFA, BFA
120 UG/60 G
4 UG
All students/4
1 FT
7 UG
NASAD

University of Michigan
School of Art

Graphic Design
2000 Bonisteel Blvd.
Ann Arbor, MI 48109
313-764-0397

Public university
BFA, MFA
128 UG
3 UG/2 G
Some students
5 FT
65 UG/4 G
NASAD

Wayne State University
College of Fine,Performing & Comm. Arts

Department of Art & Art History
Graphic Design
150 Community Arts Building
Detroit, MI 48202
313-577-2980/313-577-5355
Area Coordinator
Public university
BFA
120 UG
4–5 UG
Some students/1 semester
1 FT
130 UG

Western Michigan University
College of Fine Arts

Department of Art
Graphic Design

Kalamazoo, MI 49008
616-387-2436
Chairperson
Public university
BA, BS, BFA, MFA
122 UG/60 G
4 UG
All students/3+
3 FT
160 UG/2 G
NASAD

College of Associated Arts

344 Summit Ave.
St. Paul, MN 55102
612-224-3416/612-224-8854
Director
Private college
BFA
125 UG
4 UG
Some students/4–6
2 FT
80 UG
NATTS

Mankato State University
College of Arts & Humanities

Department of Art
Graphic Design
MSU Box 42
Mankato, MN 56001-8400
507-389-6412
Head
Public university
BA, BFA
192 UG/45 G
4 UG/1–2 G
Some students/3
1 FT
40 UG/1 G
NASAD

Minneapolis College of Art and Design

Division of Design

2510 Stevens Avenue
Minneapolis, MN 55404
612-874-7000/612-874-3704
Chairperson
Private college
BFA
120 UG
4 UG
Some students/None
8 FT
210 UG
NASAD

Moorehead State University

Department of Art
Graphic Design
Moorehead
Moorehead, MN 56563
218-236-4627
Head
Public university
BFA, MA
234 UG/48 G
5 UG/2 G
All students/3–6
2 FT
60 UG
NASAD

St. Olaf College
Art Department

Art Studio/ Art History Major

1510 St. Olaf Ave.
Northfield, MN 55057-1098
507-464-3248
Chairman
Private college
BA, BS
35 UG
2–4 UG
Some students(4)/6 mos.-1 yr
1 FT

Central Missouri State University
College of Arts and Sciences

Department of Art
Commercial Art
Art Center
Warrensburg, MO 64093
816-543-4481
Director
Public university
BFA
124 UG
4 UG
Some students
3 FT
200 UG
NASAD

Drury College

Department of Art and Art History
Visual Communication
900 N. Benton
Springfield, MO 65802
417-865-8731
Director
Private college
BA Studio Art; BA Art History
124 UG
4 UG
All students/15 Weeks
1 FT
21 UG
NCAA

College of the Ozarks

Art Department
Graphic Design
Point Lookout, MO 65726

417-334-6411/417-335-2618

Private college
BA, DS
42 UG
4 UG
3–4
1 FT
10 UG
NCAA

Stephens College

School of the Arts
Art Area
Graphics Sequence
1200 East Broadway
Columbia, MO 65215

Private college
BA, BS, BFA

4 UG
Some students/3–6
1 FT
3–10 UG

A–associate UG–undergraduate G–graduate FT–full-time PT–part-time

Title of institution	**Washington University**	**Elizabeth City State University (UNC)**
College title		
School title	School of Fine Arts	
Department title	Graphic Communications	Art
Program title	Graphic Design Communications	
Address	One Brookings Dr., Campus Box 1031 St. Louis, MO 63130	1704 Weeksville Road Elizabeth City, NC 27909
Phone/Fax	314-935-8400/314-935-8412	919-335-3347
Coordinator's title		Chairperson
Type of institution	Private university	Public university
Degrees offered	BFA	BA
Total degree credits req'd	128 UG	124 UG
Total years req'd	2 UG	4 UG
Internship/Duration (in months)		Some students/3
Number of faculty	4 FT	1 FT
Number of students	25 UG	10 UG
Accredited	NASAD, Nor	NACATE, SA

Title of institution	**Webster College**	**Fayetteville State University**
College title		College of Arts & Sciences
School title	School of Fine Arts	
Department title	Art Department	Fine Arts
Program title	Graphic Design	Visual Arts
Address	470 East Lockwood St. Louis, MO 63119	1200 Murchison Rd. Fayetteville, NC 28301
Phone/Fax	314-968-7171	919-486-1116
Coordinator's title	Chairperson	Chairperson
Type of institution	Private college	Public university
Degrees offered	BA, BFA	BA in Visual Arts (Graphic Concentration)
Total degree credits req'd	128 UG	120 UG
Total years req'd	4 UG	4 UG
Internship/Duration (in months)	Some students	Some students/4
Number of faculty	1 FT	1.5 FT
Number of students	40 UG	
Accredited		SACS

Title of institution	**Jackson State University**	**Meredith College**
College title		
School title	Liberal Arts	
Department title	Art	Art
Program title	Graphic Design	Graphic Design
Address	1400 Lynch St. Jackson, MS 39283	3800 Hillborough Street Raleigh, NC 27607-5298
Phone/Fax	601-968-2040	919-829-8432/919-829-2828
Coordinator's title	Chairperson	
Type of institution	Public university	Private college
Degrees offered	BA	BA of Arts, Science, Music, Graduate Degrees
Total degree credits req'd	132 UG	124 UG
Total years req'd	4 UG	3 UG
Internship/Duration (in months)	All students/4	All students (if elected)/4–8
Number of faculty	7 FT	2 FT
Number of students	61 UG	18 UG
Accredited	NASAD	SACS

Title of institution	**University of Southern Mississippi**	**North Carolina Central University**
College title	College of the Arts	College of Arts and Sciences
School title		Fine Arts
Department title	Department of Art	Department of Art
Program title	BFA	Graphic Design
Address	S.S. Box 5033 Hathesburgh, MS 39406	Box 19555 Durham, NC 27707
Phone/Fax	601-266-4972/601-266-5800	919-560-6391/919-560-6012
Coordinator's title		Chairperson
Type of institution	Public university	Public university
Degrees offered	BFA	BA Degree
Total degree credits req'd	133 UG	
Total years req'd	4 UG	
Internship/Duration (in months)		One semester
Number of faculty	2 FT	4 FT
Number of students	60 UG	50 UG
Accredited	NASAD	NASAD

Title of institution	**Montana State University**	**North Carolina State University**
College title	College of Arts & Architecture	
School title	School of Art	School of Design
Department title	Graphic Design Area	Department of Graphic Design
Program title		Graphic Design
Address	Haynes Hall, School of Art Bozeman, MT 59717	Box 7701 Raleigh, NC 27695
Phone/Fax	406-994-4502	919-515-2202/919-515-7330
Coordinator's title	Co-Chairman	Head
Type of institution	Public university	Public university
Degrees offered	BA	MA Graphic Design, BA Environmental Design
Total degree credits req'd	128 UG	130 UG/48 G
Total years req'd	3 UG	4 UG/2–4 G
Internship/Duration (in months)	Some students/Varies	Some students/3–6
Number of faculty	3 FT	7 FT
Number of students	160 UG	90 UG/35 G
Accredited	NASAD	

Title of institution	**Barton College**	**Western Carolina University**
College title		College of Arts & Sciences
School title		
Department title	Communication and Performing Visual Arts	Department of Art
Program title	Graphic Design	Graphic Design
Address	College Station Wilson, NC 27893	Belk Bldg. Cullonhee, NC 28723
Phone/Fax	919-399-6477/919-237-4957	704-227-7210/704-227-7705
Coordinator's title	Chairperson	Coordinator
Type of institution	Private college	Public university
Degrees offered	BS, BFA, BA	BFA, MA
Total degree credits req'd	127 UG	128 UG/33 G
Total years req'd	4 UG	3 UG/1.5 G
Internship/Duration (in months)	Some students/4	All students/3–6
Number of faculty	6 FT	2 FT
Number of students	70 UG	70 UG/4 G
Accredited		

A–associate UG–undergraduate G–graduate FT–full-time PT–part-time

Concordia College

Art
Commercial Art
800 North Columbia
Seward, NE 68434
402-643-3651
Director
Private college
BFA
72 UG
4 UG
Some students/3
3 FT
35 UG

Notre Dame College

Art Department
Graphic Communications
2321 Elm St.
Manchester, NH 03104
603-669-4298
Chairperson
Private college
BA (Comm. Art), BFA
124 UG
4 UG
All students/4
3 FT
98 UG

Franklin Pierce College
4 Year Liberal Arts College

Graphic Communications

College Road, Box 60
Rindge, NH 03461
603-899-4201/603-899-4308
Coordinator
Private college
BA
128 UG
4 UG
All students/240 hrs.
3 FT
70 UG
New England

River College

Department of Art and Music
Design
420 South Main Street
Nashua, NH 03060
603-888-1311 x276
Chairperson
Private college
BFA (Design Concentration in Comm.)
130 UG
4 UG
All students/4
2.5 FT
25 UG
New England

Jersey City State College

School of Arts & Sciences
Department of Art
Comm. Design & Technology Specialization
2039 Kennedy Blvd.
Jersey City, NJ 07305
201-200-3214/201-200-2352
Chairperson
Public college
BA, BFA, MA
128 UG/39 G
4 UG/2 G
All students/4–8
1 FT
190 UG/10 G
NASAD

Kean College of New Jersey

School of Liberal Arts
Fine Arts
Visual Communications
Morris Avenue
Union, NJ 07083
908-527-2307
Coordinator
Public college
BFA
130 UG
4 UG
Some students/Varies
6 FT
240 UG

Montclair State

School of Fine & Performing Arts
Fine Arts Department
Graphic Design
Calcia Fine Arts Building #111
Upper Montclair, NJ 07043
201-893-4307/201-893-5279
Coordinator
Public college
BA, BFA
128 UG
4 UG
Some students/4–8
1 FT
57 UG
NASAD

Rutgers University
Camden College of Arts & Sciences

Department of Art and Art History
Graphic Design and Computer Design
Fine Arts Building
Camden, NJ 08102
609-757-6176
Chairperson
Public university
BA
126 UG
4 UG
All students/3.5
2 FT
60 UG
NASAD

Rutgers University
Newark College of Arts & Sciences

Visual & Performing Arts
Art & Design
University Heights Bradley Hall
Newark, NJ 07102
201-648-5600/201-648-1392
Head
Public university
BS-124, BFA-129
129 UG
3 UG
Some students/1–2
2.5 FT
70 UG
MSAA

William Patterson College

300 Pompton Ave.
Wayne, NJ 07470
201-595-2401/201-595-3273
Professor
Private college
BFA

Some students/3
7 FT
Varies

New Mexico State University
Arts and Sciences

Art
Graphic Design
Box 30001
Las Cruces, NM 88003-0001
505-646-1705
Head
Public university
BA, BFA, MA, MFA
128 UG
4 UG/3 G

1 FT
10–15 UG/4 G
NCAC

Alfred University
New York State College of Ceramics
School of Art & Design

Main Street
Alfred, NY 14802
607-871-2412
Chairperson
Public university
BFA

2.5 UG
Some students
2 FT
6 UG
NASAD

Cazenovia College

Advertising/ Graphic Design

Seminary St.
Cazenovia, NY 13035
315-655-9446/315-655-2190
Director
Private college

120 UG
2 UG
Some students/1.5
3 FT
12 UG
MSAA

College of New Rochelle

Graduate Art Dept.
MA in Studio Art-Graphic Design
College of New Rochelle Chidwick 204
New Rochelle, NY 10805
914-654-5279/914-654-5290
Director
Private college
MS in Studio Art-Graphic Design
36 G
1.5 G
All students/180 hours
2 FT
10 G
MSAA

Daemen College

Graphic Design

4380 Main St.
Amherst, NY 14226-3592
716-839-8241/716-839-8516
Chairperson
Private college
Graphic Design BFA, Illustration BFA
122 UG
4 UG
Some students/Open
2 FT
30 UG

Hofstra University
Hofstra College of Liberal Arts & Sciences

Department of Fine Arts & Art History
Graphic Design
1000 Fulton Ave.
Hempstead, NY 11550
516-463-5474
Professor
Private university
BA, BS
129 UG
4 UG
Some students/4
1 FT
30 UG

Long Island University
C.W. Post Campus

Art Department
Graphic Design Program

Brookville, NY 11548
516-299-2464
Chairperson
Private university
BA, BFA, MA, MFA
136 UG/36 G
4 UG/2 G
All students/5+
3 FT
80 UG/3 G
NASAD

Long Island University
Southampton Campus

Fine Arts
BFA in Graphic Design
Long Island Univ., Southampton Campus
Southampton, NY 11968
516-283-4000
Director
Private university
BFA in Graphic Design, BFA in Comm. Arts
128 UG
4 UG
All students/2–4
1 FT
20 UG

Title of institution	**Manhattanville College**	**SUNY College at New Paltz**
College title		
School title		
Department title	Studio Art Dept.	Art Studio
Program title		Graphic Design
Address	125 Purchase St. Purchase, NY 10577	106 Smiley Art Bldg. New Paltz, NY 12561
Phone/Fax	914-694-2200	914-257-3830
Coordinator's title	Chairperson	Head
Type of institution	Private college	Public college
Degrees offered	BA, BFA, MAT	BFA, BS
Total degree credits req'd	120 UG/37 G	
Total years req'd	4 UG/2+ G	
Internship/Duration (in months)		Some students/4
Number of faculty	Part-Time	
Number of students		
Accredited		NASAD

Title of institution	**Mercy College**	**School of Visual Arts**
College title		
School title		
Department title	Dept. of Music & Art	Graphic Design & Advertising
Program title	BFA in Graphic Design	
Address	555 Broadway Dobbs Ferry, NY 10522	209 E. 23rd St. New York, NY 10010
Phone/Fax	914-693-4500/914-693-4351	212-679-7350/212-725-3587
Coordinator's title	Director	Chair
Type of institution	Private college	Private college
Degrees offered	BFA, BS, BA	BFA, MFA
Total degree credits req'd	120 UG	128 UG/64 G
Total years req'd	4 UG	3 UG/2 G
Internship/Duration (in months)	All students/12	Some students/4 terms
Number of faculty	2 FT	25 FT
Number of students	30 UG	355 UG/40 G
Accredited	MSAA	NASAD

Title of institution	**Parsons School of Design**	**Skidmore College**
College title		
School title		
Department title		Department of Art
Program title	Communication Design	Concentration in Graphic Arts, Major in Art
Address	66 Fifth Ave. New York, NY 10011	North Broadway Saratoga Springs, NY 12866
Phone/Fax	212-229-8910/212-229-8975	518-584-5000/518-584-3023
Coordinator's title	Chairperson	
Type of institution	Private college	Private college
Degrees offered	BFA	BS, Art (Studio)
Total degree credits req'd	134 UG	120 UG
Total years req'd	4 UG	4 UG
Internship/Duration (in months)	Some students/by semester	Some students/varies
Number of faculty	2 FT	1 FT
Number of students	287 UG	
Accredited	NASAD	NASAD

Title of institution	**Pratt Institute**	**SUNYCollege at Fredonia**
College title		
School title	School of Art & Design	
Department title	Communications Design	Department of Art
Program title		Program in Graphic Design
Address	Rm. 330 Main Bldg., Pratt Inst., 200 Willoughby, Brooklyn, NY 11205	Rockefeller Art Center Fredonia, NY 14063
Phone/Fax	718-636-3594/718-622-6174	716-673-3538/716-673-3433
Coordinator's title	Chair	Director
Type of institution	Private college	Public college
Degrees offered	BFA Communications Design	BA, BFA
Total degree credits req'd	134 UG/48–64 G	122 UG
Total years req'd	4 UG/2 G	4 UG
Internship/Duration (in months)	Some students/Open	Some students/3
Number of faculty	5 FT	2.5 FT
Number of students	300 UG/180 G	58 UG
Accredited	NASAD, MSAA	MSAA

Title of institution	**Queens College**	**Syracuse University**
College title	City University of New York	College of Visual & Performing Arts
School title		School of Art & Design
Department title		Department of Visual Communication
Program title	Art	Communications Design
Address	65–30 Kissena Boulevard Flushing, NY 11367-1597	102 Shaffer Syracuse, NY 13244-1210
Phone/Fax	718-997-4800	315-443-4071
Coordinator's title		Coordinator
Type of institution	Public university	Private university
Degrees offered	BA /BFA	BFA
Total degree credits req'd		129 UG
Total years req'd	4 UG	3 UG
Internship/Duration (in months)		Per Semester
Number of faculty	2 FT	4 FT
Number of students	10 UG	100 UG
Accredited	MSAA	NASAD

Title of institution	**SUNY at Binghamton**	**College of Saint Rose**
College title	Harpur	
School title		School of Arts & Humanities
Department title	Art & Art History	Department of Art
Program title	Design	Graphic Design Program
Address	Vestal Parkway Binghamton, NY 13902	432 Western Ave. Albany, NY 12203
Phone/Fax		518-485-3900/518-438-3293
Coordinator's title	Chairperson	Assoc. Prof.
Type of institution	Public college	Private college
Degrees offered	BA, BFA	BS in Graphic Design
Total degree credits req'd		122 UG
Total years req'd	4 UG	4 UG
Internship/Duration (in months)	All students	Some students/12
Number of faculty	2 FT	3 FT
Number of students	20 UG	65 UG
Accredited		NASAD

A–associate UG–undergraduate G–graduate FT–full-time PT–part-time

Cooper Union for the Advancement of Science & Art
The School of Art
Graphic Design
Bachelor of Fine Arts
41 Cooper Square
New York, NY 10003
212-353-4200/212-353-4345
Acting Dean
Private college
BFA
128 UG
3 UG
Some students

NASAD, MSAA

New School/Parsons School of Design

Communication Design
BFA
66 Fifth Avenue/2 W. 13th St.
New York, NY 10011
212-229-8910/212-229-8975
Chairperson
Private college
BFA
134 UG
3 UG
Some students/1
2 FT/45 PT
287 UG
NASAD, Mid

SUNY College at Buffalo

Arts & Letters
Department of Art
Communication Design
2917 Main Street , 303 Bethune Hall
Buffalo, NY 14214
716-831-3477/716-831-2392
Director
Public university
BFA, BA, MFA
128 UG/60 G
4 UG/2 G
Some students/One Semester
3 FT
30 UG/4 G
NASAD

College of Mount St. Joseph

Department of Art
Graphic Design
5701 Delhi Rd.
Cincinnati, OH 45233-1607
513-244-4420/513-244-4222
Head
Private college
BA, BFA, AS
128 UG
4 UG
All students
1 FT
75 UG
NCAA

Bowling Green State University
College of Arts & Sciences
School of Art
Design Division
Graphic Design
Fine Arts Center
Bowling Green, OH 43403-0211
419-372-2640/419-372-2544

Public university
BFA, MFA
122 UG/61–62 G
4 UG
Some students
3 FT
213 UG/1 G
NASAD

Cleveland Institute of Art

Graphic Design

11141 E. Blvd.
Cleveland, OH 44106
216-421-7300/216-421-7438
Chair
Private college
BFA
179 UG
3 UG
Some students/8
4.2 FT
51 UG
NASAD, NCAA

Miami University

School of Fine Arts
Department of Art
Graphic Design
124 Art Bldg.
Oxford, OH 45056
513-529-2900/513-529-3841

Public university
BFA
128 UG
4 UG
Some students/3
3 FT
80 UG
NASAD

Ohio University
College of Fine Arts
School of Art
Graphic Design
Graphic Design (Design or Illus. Emphasis)
School of Art, Seigfred Hall, Ohio Univ.
Athens, OH 45701-2979
614-593-4288/614-593-0457
Area Representative
Public university
BFA
192 UG
4 UG

4 FT
27 UG

Columbus College of Art & Design

Admissions Office

107 N. 9th St.
Columbus, OH 43215
614-224-9101/614-222-4040

Private college
BA
145 UG
4.5 UG
No students
15 FT
230 UG
NASAD

Ohio State University
College of the Arts
DNA
Department of Industrial Design
Visual Communication
380 Hopkins Hall, 128 N. Oval Mall
Columbus, OH 43210
614-292-6746/614-292-7641

Public university
BSID, MA
195 UG/60 G
4 UG/2 G
Some students/3
5 FT
60 UG/8 G
FIDER

University of Akron
Fine & Applied Arts
School of Art

Bachelor of Fine Arts in Graphic Design
Folk Hall
Akron, OH 44325
216-972-6030/216-972-5959
Director
Public university
BFA, BA

4 UG
Some students/Varies
10 FT
247 UG
NASAD

University of Cincinnati
Col. of Des., Architecture, Art & Planning
School of Design
Graphic Design

Cincinnati, OH 45221-0016
513-556-6828
Chairperson
Public university
BS in Design, Master of Design
199 UG
5 UG/2 G
All students/18
6 FT
200–250 UG/4 G
NASAD

University of Dayton
Arts & Sciences

Visual Arts
Visual Communication Design
300 College Park
Dayton, OH 45469-1690
513-229-3220
Area Coordinator
Private university
BFA
129 UG
4–5 UG
Some students/4
5 FT
115 UG

Wittenberg University

Art Department
Graphic Design
Box 720
Springfield, OH 45501
513-327-6311
Professor
Private university
BA, BFA
150 UG
3 UG
Some students/3
5 FT
13 UG
NCAA

Youngstown State University
College of Fine & Performing Arts

Art Department
Graphic Design
410 Wick Ave.
Youngstown, OH 44555
216-742-3627/216-742-1419
Coordinator
Public university
BFA, AAB
186+ UG
4+ UG
Some students/6
3 FT
180 UG

Oklahoma Baptist University
College of Fine Arts

Art Department

500 W. University
Shawnee, OK 74801
405-275-2810
Chairperson
Private university
BA, BFA
120 UG
4 UG

Oklahoma State University
Arts & Sciences

Art
Graphic Design
108 Bartlett Center
Stillwater, OK 74078-0120
405-744-6016

Public university
BFA
138 UG
4–5 UG
Some students/3–6
2 FT
100 UG

Southwestern Oklahoma State Univ.
Arts & Sciences
Art
Commercial

100 Campus Drive
Weatherford, OK 73096
405-774-3756

Public university
BA Com, BA Art Ed, MA Art Ed, BA Fine Art
124 UG/45 G
4–5 UG/2 G
Some students/1–12
1 FT
40 UG
NCAA

A–associate UG–undergraduate G–graduate FT–full-time PT–part-time

Title of institution	**University of Tulsa**	**University of Oregon**
College title	Kendell College of Arts and Sciences	
School title	School of Arts	Architecture & Allied Arts
Department title		Fine & Applied Arts
Program title	Graphic Design	Visual Design–Graphics
Address	Phillips Hall, 600 S. College Tulsa, OK 74104	190 Lawrence Hall Eugene, OR 97403
Phone/Fax	918-631-2200/918-631-2033	503-346-3610/503-346-3660
Coordinator's title	Director	Coordinator
Type of institution	Private university	Public university
Degrees offered	BA, BFA, MA, MTA, MFA	BA, BS, BFA, MFA
Total degree credits req'd	124 UG/30–60 G	66 UG
Total years req'd	4 UG	4–5 UG/2–3 G
Internship/Duration (in months)	All students/3–6	Some students
Number of faculty	1.5 FT	4 FT
Number of students	15 UG/2 G	100 UG/5 G
Accredited		NASAD

Title of institution	**University of Oklahoma**	**Kent State University**
College title	College of Fine Arts	College of Fine and Professional Arts
School title	School of Art	School of Art
Department title		Division of Design
Program title	Visual Communication	Graphic Design and Illustration
Address	520 Parrington Oval, Rm. 202 Norman, OK 73019	Kent, OH 44242
Phone/Fax	405-325-6991/405-325-1668	216-672-2192
Coordinator's title		Coordinator
Type of institution	Public university	Public university
Degrees offered	BFA, MFA	BFA, MA, MFA
Total degree credits req'd	124 UG/60 G	129 UG/32–60 G
Total years req'd	4+ UG/2+ G	4.5 UG
Internship/Duration (in months)	Some students/3–6	All students/1.5–2
Number of faculty	3 FT	7 FT
Number of students	120–130 UG/4+ G	475 UG/12–15 G
Accredited		NASAD

Title of institution	**Oregon State University**	**Miami University**
College title	Liberal Arts	
School title		School of Fine Arts
Department title	Department of Art	Department of Art
Program title		Graphic Design Area
Address	Fairbanks 106 Corvallis, OR 97331	Oxford, OH 45056
Phone/Fax	503-737-4745/503-737-2434	513-529-2900/513-529-3841
Coordinator's title	Chair	Head
Type of institution	Public university	Public university
Degrees offered	BA, BS, BFA	BFA
Total degree credits req'd	192 UG	128 UG
Total years req'd	4 UG	4 UG
Internship/Duration (in months)	Some students/2–3	Some students/3
Number of faculty	4 FT	3 FT
Number of students	180 UG	75 UG
Accredited		NASAD

Title of institution	**Pacific Northwest College of Art**	**Ohio State University**
College title		College of the Arts
School title		
Department title	Design Arts	Department of Industrial Design
Program title		Visual Communication
Address	1219 S.W. Park Ave. Portland, OR 97205	380 Hopkins Hall, 128 N. Oval Mall Columbus, OH 43210
Phone/Fax	503-226-4391/503-226-4842	614-292-6746
Coordinator's title	Chairperson	Head
Type of institution	Private college	Public university
Degrees offered	BFA	BSID
Total degree credits req'd	122 UG	195 UG/60 G
Total years req'd	4 UG	4 UG/2 G
Internship/Duration (in months)	All students/3	Some students/1 semester
Number of faculty	1.4 FT	6 FT
Number of students	18.7 UG	75 UG/5 G
Accredited	NASAD, NCAA	NASAD

Title of institution	**Portland Art Museum**	**York University**
College title	Pacific Northwest College of Art	Faculty of Fine Arts
School title		
Department title	Design Arts	Department of Visual Art
Program title	Graphic Design	Visual Communication Design Area
Address	1219 S.W. Park Ave. Portland, OR 97205	4700 Keele Street Toronto, Ontario, Canada M3J 1P3
Phone/Fax	503-226-0462	416-736-5187/416-736-5447
Coordinator's title	Chairperson	Area Representative
Type of institution	Private school	Public university
Degrees offered	BFA	BA in Art & Design History/Theory BFA
Total degree credits req'd	122 UG	20 UG/5 G
Total years req'd	3 UG	4 UG
Internship/Duration (in months)	All students/4	Some students/4
Number of faculty	2 FT	3 FT
Number of students	30 UG	120 UG/4 G
Accredited	NASAD	NASAD

Title of institution	**Portland State University**	**Mount Aloysius College**
College title	School of Fine & Performing Arts	
School title		
Department title	Department of Art	Art
Program title	Graphic Design	
Address	Box 751 Portland, OR 97207	1 College Dr. Cresson, PA 16630-1999
Phone/Fax	503-725-3515	
Coordinator's title	Head	
Type of institution	Public university	College
Degrees offered	BA, BS	BFA
Total degree credits req'd	186 UG	
Total years req'd	4 UG	
Internship/Duration (in months)	Some students/6	
Number of faculty	2.5 FT	
Number of students	150 UG	
Accredited	NASAD	

A—associate UG—undergraduate G—graduate FT—full-time PT—part-time

Seton Hill College

Art
Graphic Design

Greensburg, PA 15601
412-834-2200, x399
Chairperson
Private college
BFA, BA
64 UG
4 UG
All students/3–6
3 FT
33 UG

Moravian College

Art Department
Graphic and Advertising Design
Church Street Campus
Bethlehem, PA 18018
215-861-1680
Head
Private college
BA
126 UG
4 UG
All students/4
1 FT
44 UG
Middle States

Beaver College

Department of Fine Arts
Bachelor of Fine Arts
Church and Easton Rds.
Glenside, PA 19038
215-572-2133
Head
Private college
BFA, BA
128 UG
4 UG
Some students/15 weeks
1.33 FT
40 UG
NASAD

Carnegie Mellon University
College of Fine Arts

Department of Design
Graphic Design Program

Pittsburgh, PA 15213
412-268-2828/412-268-3088
Head
Private university
BFA
384 UG
4 UG
Some students/6
5 FT
70+ UG
NASAD

Drexel University
College of Design Arts

Interiors and Graphic Studies Dept.
Graphic Design
32nd & Market Streets
Philadelphia, PA 19104
215-895-2390/215-895-4917
Program Head
Private university
BS in Graphic Design
180 UG
4 UG
All students/9
4.5 FT
120 UG
Middle States

Edinboro University of Pennsylvania

Art Department
Communication Graphics
102 Doucette Hall
Edinboro, PA 16444
814-732-2406
Director
Public university
BFA, Applied Media Arts BFA
128 UG
3–4 UG
All students/1 semester
3 FT
360 UG
Middle States

Marywood College

Department of Art
Graphic Design, Advertising Graphics Prog.
2300 Adams Avenue
Scranton, PA 18509
717-348-6211
Head
Private college
BFA, MA, MFA
130 UG, 60 G
4 UG
All students/1–2 semesters
3 FT
75 UG/Varies G
NASAD

Indiana University of Pennsylvania
College of Fine Arts

Department of Art
FA Art Studio: Graphic Design
405 Sprowls Hall, Indiana Univ. of PA
Indiana, PA 15705
412-357-2530

Public university
BFA Studio; BS Art Education
124 UG
4 UG
All students/1 semester
1 FT
20 UG
Middle States

Kutztown University
College of Visual & Performing Arts

Communication Design
Bachelor of Fine Arts: Comm. Design
University House
Kutztown, PA 19530
215-683-4530/215-683-4547
Chairperson
Public university
BFA
128 UG
4 UG
Some students
10 FT
330 UG

Lycoming College

Art
Commercial Design
700 College Pl.
Williamsport, PA 17701
717-321-4002
Chairperson
Private college
BA
128 UG
4 UG
4
2 FT
15 UG

Mansfield University

Art
Advertising, Design and Lettering
Allen Hall
Mansfield, PA 16933
717-662-4500
Chairperson
Public university
BA
140 UG
4–5 UG

34 FT

Middle States

Mercy Hurst College

Art Department

Glenwoods Hills
Erie, PA 16415
814-824-2384/814-824-2438

Private university
BA in Art, Education, Art Therapy
120 UG
4 UG
Some students/3
1 FT
10 UG

Messiah College

Visual & Theatrical Arts
Graphic Design

Grantham, PA 17027
717-766-2511/717-691-6046
Head
Private college
BA
126 UG
4 UG
All students
1.5 FT
30 UG

Moore College of Art & Design

Graphic Design

20th Street & Benjamin Franklin Parkway
Philadelphia, PA 19103-1179
215-568-4515/215-568-4963 or 8017
Chairperson
Private college
BFA in Graphic Design
126.5 UG
4 UG
All students/2 months
2 FT
62 UG
NASAD

Penn State University
College of Art and Architecture
School of Visual Arts

Graphic Design
102 Visual Arts Building
University Park, PA 16802
814-865-0444/814-865-7140
Head
Public university
BFA, BA
124 UG/60 G
3 UG/2 G
Some students/Varies
4 FT
48 UG/2 G
NASAD

Temple University
Tyler School of Art

Graphic Arts & Design
Visual Design
Beech & Penrose Aves.
Elkins Park, PA 19126
215-782-2869/215-782-2799
Chairperson
University
BFA, MFA
132 UG/60 G
2 UG/2 G

11 FT
120 UG/10 G
NASAD

University of the Arts
Philadelphia College of Art & Design

Graphic Design

Broad & Pine Streets
Philadelphia, PA 19102
215-875-1060
Chairperson
Private university
BFA
132 UG
3 UG

7 FT
87 UG
NASAD

University of Pittsburgh

Studio Art Department
Studio Arts
104 Frick Fine Arts Building
Pittsburgh, PA 15260
412-648-2430/412-648-2792
Chairperson
Public university
BA in Studio Art
120 UG
4 UG
Some students/3
1 PT

A—associate UG—undergraduate G—graduate FT—full time PT—part time

Title of institution	**Washington and Jefferson College**	**Bob Jones University**
College title		
School title		School of Fine Arts
Department title	Art Department	Division of Art
Program title		Graphic Design
Address	Olin Fine Arts Center Washington, PA 15301	Bob Jones University Greenville, SC 29614
Phone/Fax	412-222-4400	803-242-5100 x1250/803-242-5100
Coordinator's title	Chairperson	Chair
Type of institution	Private college	Private university
Degrees offered		BS
Total degree credits req'd	36 UG	128 UG
Total years req'd	4 UG	4 UG
Internship/Duration (in months)		All students/4
Number of faculty		3 FT
Number of students		66 UG
Accredited		

Title of institution	**Waynesburg College**	**University of South Carolina**
College title		College of Humanities & Social Services
School title		Sloan College
Department title	Fine Arts	Department of Art
Program title	Visual Communication	Graphic Design Division
Address	51 W. College St. Waynesburg, PA 15370	 Columbia, SC 29208
Phone/Fax	412-852-2304	803-777-4236/803-777-9558
Coordinator's title	Chairperson	Head
Type of institution	Private college	Public university
Degrees offered	BA, Associate	BFA, BA
Total degree credits req'd	124 UG	120 UG
Total years req'd	2–4 UG	3 UG
Internship/Duration (in months)	All students/200 hours	Some students/Varies
Number of faculty	1.5 FT	3–5 FT
Number of students	45 UG	90 UG
Accredited		

Title of institution	**Rhode Island College**	**Augustana College**
College title		
School title		
Department title	Art	Art
Program title	Graphic Design	Graphic Design
Address	600 Mt. Pleasant Ave. Providence, RI 02908	29th and Summit Sioux Falls, SD 57102
Phone/Fax	401-456-8054	502-336-5425
Coordinator's title	Chairperson	Director
Type of institution	Public college	
Degrees offered	BA, BFA, MA	BA
Total degree credits req'd	120 UG/60 G	120 UG
Total years req'd	4 UG	4 UG
Internship/Duration (in months)	Some students/3	Some students
Number of faculty	2 FT	1 FT
Number of students	100 UG/2 G	25 UG
Accredited	NASAD	

Title of institution	**Rhode Island School of Design**	**South Dakota State University**
College title		College of Arts & Sciences
School title	Division of Design & Architecture	South Dakota State University
Department title	Graphic Design Department	Visual Arts Dept.
Program title		Graphic Design
Address	2 College St. Providence, RI 02903	103-Silberg Hall Brookings, SD 57006
Phone/Fax	401-454-6171/401-454-6320	605-688-4103
Coordinator's title	Head	Chair
Type of institution	Private college	Public university
Degrees offered	BFA, BGD, MFA	BA, BS
Total degree credits req'd	156 UG/66 G	128 UG
Total years req'd	3–4 UG/2 G	4 UG
Internship/Duration (in months)	Some students/6 wks.	Some students/3
Number of faculty	11 PT	2.5 FT
Number of students	188 UG/16 G	45 UG
Accredited	NASAD	

Title of institution	**Coker College**	**University of South Dakota**
College title		College of Fine Art
School title		
Department title	Art Department	Art
Program title	Graphic Design	Graphics
Address	College Avenue Hartsville, SC 29550	414 East Clark Street Vermillion, SD 57069-2390
Phone/Fax	803-383-8150	605-677-5636
Coordinator's title	Chairperson	
Type of institution	Private college	
Degrees offered	BA	BFA, Art Graphics
Total degree credits req'd	120 UG	128 UG
Total years req'd	4 UG	4–5 UG
Internship/Duration (in months)	Some Students/Variable	Some students/3–5
Number of faculty	1 FT	1 FT
Number of students	10 UG	
Accredited		NASAD

Title of institution	**Anderson College**	**Austin Peay State University**
College title		
School title		
Department title	Art	Department of Art
Program title	Graphic Design	Art Major, Graphic Design
Address	316 Blvd. Anderson, SC 29621	Box 4677, Dept. of Art, Clarksville, TN 37044
Phone/Fax	803-231-2000/803-231-2004	615-648-7333/615-648-7475
Coordinator's title	Coordinator	Chairperson
Type of institution	Private college	Public university
Degrees offered	BA	BFA, BA, BS
Total degree credits req'd	128 UG	138 UG
Total years req'd	4 UG	4.5 UG
Internship/Duration (in months)	All students/4	Some students/8
Number of faculty	1 FT	1.5 FT
Number of students	25 UG	60 UG
Accredited		NASAD

A—associate UG—undergraduate G—graduate FT—full time PT—part time

East Tennessee State University
College of Arts & Sciences

Art Department
Graphic Design BFA, MFA
Box 70708
Johnson City, TN 37604
615-929-4247
Chair
Public university
BFA, MFA
128 UG/60 G
5 UG/3 G
Some students/3–6
2 FT
70 UG/1 G
NASAD

Memphis College of Art

Design Arts BFA/Visual Info. Arts MFA

Overton Park
Memphis, TN 38112
901-726-4085/901-726-9371
Chairperson
Private
BFA, MFA

4 UG/2 G
All students
6.5 FT
100 UG/15 G
NASAD, SAC

Memphis State University
College of Communication & Fine Arts

Department of Art
Graphic Design
Jones Hall 201
Memphis, TN 38152
901-678-2216/901-678-3299

Public university
MFA, BFA
142hr UG/60hr G
4 UG/3 G
Some students/3
4 FT
130 UG/10 G
NASAD

University of Tennessee at Chattanooga
College of Arts & Sciences

Art
G. Des. (Art Ed., Painting, Drawing, Sculp.)
615 McCallie Ave.
Chattanooga, TN 37403
615-755-4178
Head
Public university
BA, BFA
128 UG
4 UG
All students (Graphic Design)/4
3 FT
75 UG
NASAD (pending)

University of Tennessee at Knoxville
College of Liberal Arts

Department of Art
Graphic Design/Illustration Programs
1715 Volunteer Blvd.
Knoxville, TN 37996
615-974-3408
Head
Public university
BA, BFA, MFA
128 UG/60 G
4 UG/3 G
Some students/2–12
6 FT
250 UG/7 G
NASAD

Angelo State University
College of Liberal & Fine Arts

Department of Art & Music

2601 W. Ave. N
San Angelo, TX 76909
915-942-2085/915-942-2038
Head
Public university
BA
130 UG
4 UG
All students/4
1 FT
10 UG

Dallas Baptist University

Art Department
Art
3000 Mountain Creek Pkwy.
Dallas, TX 75211-9299
214-333-5300
Chair
Private university
BA, BS, MLA
130 UG
2 UG/1 G
Some students/1–2 semesters
1 FT
10 UG

Lamar University
Fine Arts & Communication

Art
Visual Design
Box 10027
Beaumont, TX 77710
409-880-8141

Public university
BFA, MA
134 UG/36 G
4 UG/2 G

2 FT
85 UG

San Antonio Art Institute

Department of Graphic Design
Graphic Design
6000 N. New Braunfels
San Antonio, TX 78209
512-824-7224/512-824-6622
Head
Private college
BFA

4 UG
All students/Varies
1 FT
12 UG
NASAD, SAC

Texas Christian University
College of Fine Arts & Communication

Department of Art and Art History
Communication Graphics
Box 30793
Ft. Worth, TX 76129
817-921-7643/817-921-7703
Coordinator
Private university
BFA
124 UG
2 UG
Some students/2
2 FT
70 UG
SACA

Texas Tech University

Arts and Science
Art Department
Design Communication

Lubbock, TX 79409
806-742-3825
Area Representative
Public university
BFA
135 UG
4.5 UG

2 FT
200 UG
NASAD

Texas Woman's University
Arts & Sciences

Visual Arts
Advertising Design
Box 22995
Denton, TX 76204
817-898-2530
Director
Public university
BFA, MA
144 UG/30 G
4–5 UG/2 G
All students/8
2 FT
50 UG/10 G
SACS

University of Texas at El Paso
College of Liberal Arts

Department of Art
Graphic Design
500 W. Univ. St.
El Paso, TX 79968
915-747-5181

Public university
BA, BFA, MA
138 UG/36 G
4 UG/1–2 G
All students/4
1.67 FT
96 UG/1 G

University of North Texas

School of Visual Arts
Professional Design
Communication Design
Box 5098
Denton, TX 76203-5098
817-565-4001
Head
Public university
BFA, MFA Communication Design
138 UG
4–5 UG/2–3 G
Some students/3–6
8 FT
470 UG/25 G
NASAD, SAC

University of Texas at Arlington
College of Liberal Arts

Department of Art and Art History
Graphic Communication
Box 19089
Arlington, TX 76019
817-273-2891
Director
Public university
BFA
128 UG
3 UG
Some students/4
3 FT
110 UG

University of Texas at Austin
College of Fine Arts

Art
Division of Design

Austin, TX 78712
512-471-3365/512-471-7801
Director
Public University
BFA, MFA
120 UG/60 G
4 UG/2–3 G
Some students/Varies
5.5 FT
120 UG/4 G

University of Texas-Pan American

Department of Art
Advertising Art
1202 W. University Dr.
Edinburg, TX 78539
512-381-3480
Chairperson
Public university
BFA
124 UG
4 UG
Some students/4
1 FT
60 UG

West Texas State University
Fine Arts & Humanities

Art, Communication & Theatre
Graphic Design
WT Box 747
Canyon, TX 79106
806-656-2799
Head
Public university
BFA, MFA, MA
130 UG/60 G
3 UG/2 G
Some students/4
1 FT
50 UG/1 G
SACS

Title of institution	**Brigham Young University**	**Hampton University**
College title	College of Fine Arts & Communications	
School title		School of Liberal Arts & Education
Department title	Dept. of Design	Art
Program title	Graphic Design	
Address	210 BRMB Provo, UT 84602	Art Department Hampton, VA 23668
Phone/Fax	801-378-2064/801-378-2954	804-727-5416/804-727-5084
Coordinator's title	Area Coordinator	Chairperson
Type of institution	Private university	Private university
Degrees offered	BFA	BA in Art with Emphasis in Graphic Design
Total degree credits req'd	120 UG	120 UG
Total years req'd	4 UG	4 UG
Internship/Duration (in months)		Some students/Optional
Number of faculty	2 FT	1 FT
Number of students	75 UG	
Accredited		SAA

Title of institution	**Salt Lake Community College**	**James Madison University**
College title		College of Fine Arts & Communication
School title	Occupational Education	
Department title	Graphic Design Dept.	Department of Art
Program title	Graphic Design	Graphic Design
Address	4600 S. Redwood Road, Box 30808 Salt Lake City, UT 84130-0808	Harrisonburg, VA 22807
Phone/Fax	801-967-4074	703-568-6216
Coordinator's title	Coordinator	Chairperson
Type of institution	Public college	Public university
Degrees offered		BFA, BS
Total degree credits req'd	96 G	128 UG
Total years req'd	2–3 G	4 UG
Internship/Duration (in months)	Some students/3	Some students
Number of faculty	10 FT	3 FT
Number of students	112 UG	100 UG
Accredited	NWASC	NASAD

Title of institution	**University of Utah**	**Longwood College**
College title	College of Fine Arts	
School title		Liberal Arts & Sciences
Department title	Art Department	Department of Fine Arts
Program title	Graphic Design	Graphic Design
Address	161 AAC Salt Lake City, UT 84112	Art Dept. 201 High St., Farmville, VA 23909
Phone/Fax	801-581-8867	804-395-2284/804-395-2775
Coordinator's title	Head	Chairperson
Type of institution	Public university	Public college
Degrees offered	Undergraduate and MFA	BFA
Total degree credits req'd		132 UG
Total years req'd		4 UG
Internship/Duration (in months)		All students/3
Number of faculty	3 FT	2 FT
Number of students	183 UG/72 G	30 UG
Accredited	NASAD	

Title of institution	**Utah State University**	**Marymount University**
College title	Humanities, Arts & Social Sciences	
School title		Arts & Sciences
Department title	Department of Art	
Program title		Graphic Design
Address	Logan, UT 84322-4000	2807 N. Glebe Rd. Arlington, VA 22207
Phone/Fax	801-750-3460	703-284-1500
Coordinator's title	Head	Chair
Type of institution	Public university	Public university
Degrees offered	BS, BA, BFA, MA, MFA	BA
Total degree credits req'd	186 UG/90 G	120 UG
Total years req'd	4 UG/2 G	4 UG
Internship/Duration (in months)	Some students/Varies	All students
Number of faculty	2 FT	2 FT
Number of students	49 UG	60 UG
Accredited	NASC	

Title of institution	**Weber State University**	**Old Dominion University**
College title	Arts & Humanities	Arts & Letters
School title		
Department title	Visual Arts	Art
Program title	Visual Communications	Graphic Design
Address	3750 Harrison Blvd. Ogden, UT 84408-2001	Norfolk, VA 23529-0186
Phone/Fax	801-626-6455	804-683-4047/804-683-5457
Coordinator's title	Program Coordinator	
Type of institution	Public university	Public university
Degrees offered	BS, BA, BFA	BA(Studio Art) BFA, MA, MFA
Total degree credits req'd	183 UG	126 UG/60 G
Total years req'd	4 UG	4 UG/2–3 G
Internship/Duration (in months)	Some students	Some students/9
Number of faculty	1 FT	2 FT
Number of students	35 UG	70 UG/1 G
Accredited		

Title of institution	**George Mason University**	**Radford University**
College title	College of Arts and Sciences	College of Visual & Performing Arts
School title		
Department title	Department of Art and Art History	Department of Art
Program title	Art Studio (UG) Visual Info. Tech.	Graphic Design Option
Address	400 University Drive Fairfax, VA 22030	Powell Hall Radford, VA 24142
Phone/Fax	703-993-1010	703-831-5475
Coordinator's title	Chairperson	Chair
Type of institution	Public university	Public university
Degrees offered	BA, MFA	BA, BS, BFA, MS, MFA
Total degree credits req'd	120 UG/60 G	126 UG/60 G
Total years req'd	4 UG	Varies
Internship/Duration (in months)	All students/3–6	Some students/3
Number of faculty	1 FT	2 FT
Number of students	60 UG	40 UG/3 G
Accredited		

A—associate UG—undergraduate G—graduate FT—full-time PT—part-time

Virginia Commonwealth University

School of the Arts
Communication Arts & Design
Graphic Design/Visual Communications
325 No. Harrison St.
Richmond, VA 23284-2519
804-367-1709/804-367-6469
Chairperson
Public university
BFA, MFA
132 UG/60 G
4 UG/2 G
Some students
16 FT
367 UG/16 G
NASAD, SAC

Central Washington University
College of Letters, Arts & Sciences

Art Department
Graphic Design
Art Dept., Central Washington Univ.
Ellensburg, WA 98926
509-963-1544/509-963-1241
Director
Public university
BA
180 UG
4 UG
All students/2
2 FT
80 UG

Cornish College of the Arts

Design Department

710 E. Roy St.
Seattle, WA 98102
206-322-1400/206-323-1574
Chairperson
Private college
BFA
130 UG
4 UG
All students/3
13 FT
40 UG
NWASC

University of Washington
College of Arts and Sciences
School of Art
Division of Design and Photography
Graphic Design Communications
School of Art DM-10
Seattle, WA 98195
206-685-1714/206-685-1657
Chairperson
Public university
BFA/MFA in Graphic Design
198 UG/72 G
4 UG/2 G

5 FT
47 UG/5 G

Viterbo College

School of Fine Arts
Art
Art in Business
815 S. 9th Street
La Crosse, WA 54601
608-791-0330/608-791-0367
Chairperson
Private college
BS in Art in Business, BA in Studio Art
128 UG
4 UG
All students/3–6
.5 FT
40 UG

Western Washington University

Art Department
Design/Illustration
Western Washington U.
Bellingham, WA 98225-9068
206-676-3661/206-647-6878
Head
Public university
BA, BFA
80 UG/140 G
4 UG/1 G
Some students/3
5 FT
125 UG/2 G

Milwaukee Institute of Art & Design

Design Department
Graphic Design
273 E. Erie St.
Milwaukee, WI 53202-5711
414-276-7889
Head
Private college
BFA
123 UG
4 UG
Some students/4
4 FT
117 UG
NASAD

Mount Mary College

Art Department
Graphic Design
2900 N. Menomonee River Pkwy.
Milwaukee, WI 33222
414-258-4810/414-256-1205
Director
Public college
BA
128 UG
4 UG
All students/4
1 FT
50 UG

Carthage College

Graphic Design

2001 Alford Dr.
Kenosha, WI 53414
414-551-8500/414-551-6208

Private college
BA (Graphic Design)
136 UG
4 UG
All students
1 FT
40 UG

University of Wisconsin—Stout

School of Liberal Studies
Department of Art and Design
Graphic Design
Applied Arts Building
Menomonie, WI 54751
715-232-1141/715-232-1669

Public university
BFA
132 UG
3 UG
Some students/3–6
3.3 FT
195 UG
NASAD

University of Wisconsin—Eau Claire

Arts & Sciences
Department of Art
Graphic Design
Fine Arts Center
Eau Claire, WI 54701
715-836-3277
Chairperson
Public university
BA, BFA
78 UG
4 UG
Some students/3–6
2 FT
102 UG

University of Wisconsin—Oshkosh

Art Department
Graphic Comm.

Oshkosh, WI 54901
414-424-2222
Coordinator
Public university
BA, BS, BFA
82 UG
4 UG
Some students/1 semester
4 FT
240 UG

University of Wisconsin—Whitewater
College of the Arts

Art Department
Graphic Design

Whitewater, WI 53190
414-472-1324
Chair
Public university
BFA, BA
120 UG
4 UG
Some students/4
4 FT
120 UG

University of Wisconsin—Madison

School of Education
Department of Art

455 N. Park St., 6241 Humanities Bldg.
Madison, WI 53706
608-262-1660/608-262-2150

Public university
BS in Art, BFA, MA in Art, MFA
120 UG/60 G
4 UG

3.1 FT

NASAD

Bethany College

Communications
Graphic Design
Johnson Center
Bethany, WV 26032
304-829-7747
Chairperson
Private college

130 UG
4 UG
All students
3 FT
16 UG

Marshall University
College of Fine Arts

Department of Art
Graphic Design
400 Hal Greer Blvd.
Huntington, WV 25755
304-696-6760/304-696-3333
Director
Public university
BFA
138 UG
4 UG
All students/1
3 FT
114 UG
NCASC

Shepherd College

School of Arts and Humanities
Art
Graphic Design
Frank Center for Creative Art
Shepherdstown, WV 25443
304-876-2511/304-876-3101
Head
Public university
BFA, BA, AA
128 UG
4 UG
Some students
3 FT
70 UG
NCASC

West Liberty State College

Art Department
Graphic Design

West Liberty, WV 26074
304-336-8006
Head
Public college
BS, BA
128 UG
4 UG
Some students/4
1 FT
35 UG

A—associate UG—undergraduate G—graduate FT—full time PT—part time

Title of institution	**West Virginia State College**
College title	
School title	
Department title	Art
Program title	BA Art
Address	Campus Box 4, PO Box 1000 Institute, WV 25112-1000
Phone/Fax	304-766-3196/304-768-9842
Coordinator's title	Chairperson
Type of institution	Public college
Degrees offered	BA in Art
Total degree credits req'd	121 UG
Total years req'd	4 UG
Internship/Duration (in months)	
Number of faculty	.5 FT
Number of students	15 UG
Accredited	

Title of institution	**University of Wyoming**
College title	Arts & Sciences
School title	
Department title	Art
Program title	Graphic Design
Address	Art Dept., Box 3138 Laramie, WY 82071
Phone/Fax	307-766-3269
Coordinator's title	Director
Type of institution	Public university
Degrees offered	BFA in Graphic Design
Total degree credits req'd	128 UG
Total years req'd	4.5 UG
Internship/Duration (in months)	All students
Number of faculty	1.5 FT
Number of students	27 UG
Accredited	

Title of institution	
College title	
School title	
Department title	
Program title	
Address	
Phone/Fax	
Coordinator's title	
Type of institution	
Degrees offered	
Total degree credits req'd	
Total years req'd	
Internship/Duration (in months)	
Number of faculty	
Number of students	
Accredited	

Title of institution	
College title	
School title	
Department title	
Program title	
Address	
Phone/Fax	
Coordinator's title	
Type of institution	
Degrees offered	
Total degree credits req'd	
Total years req'd	
Internship/Duration (in months)	
Number of faculty	
Number of students	
Accredited	

Title of institution	
College title	
School title	
Department title	
Program title	
Address	
Phone/Fax	
Coordinator's title	
Type of institution	
Degrees offered	
Total degree credits req'd	
Total years req'd	
Internship/Duration (in months)	
Number of faculty	
Number of students	
Accredited	

Title of institution	
College title	
School title	
Department title	
Program title	
Address	
Phone/Fax	
Coordinator's title	
Type of institution	
Degrees offered	
Total degree credits req'd	
Total years req'd	
Internship/Duration (in months)	
Number of faculty	
Number of students	
Accredited	

A—associate UG—undergraduate G—graduate FT—full time PT—part time

Credits

Chapter 1

p. 8 Brad Holland, Randy Messer, Virginia Commonwealth University, Rochester Institute of Technology, Parsons School of Design, John Muller
p. 9 University of Illinois, Pennsylvania State University, Woody Pirtle, Ringling School of Art
p. 10 Mieko Oda, Richard Poulin, Tamotsu Yagi, Institute of Design, University of Cincinnati, Michael Beirut
p. 11 Art Center, Rudolph de Harak, School of Visual Arts, Charles S. Anderson
p. 12 Crit Warren, Ohio University, Rochester Institute of Technology, Art Center
p. 13 Joel Katz, University of the Arts, Byron Glaser, Sandra Higashi, April Greiman, University of Washington
p. 14 University of Cincinnati, Paul Rand, Ron Kellum, Ringling School of Art, North Carolina State University
p. 15 William Golden, Carnegie Mellon University, University of Cincinnati, Clement Mok

Chapter 2

Arizona State University, Art Center, California College of Arts and Crafts, Carnegie Mellon University, Eastern Michigan University, Institute of Design, Minnesota College of Art and Design, North Carolina State University, Ohio University, Parsons School of Design, Pennsylvania State University, Ringling School of Art, Rhode Island School of Design, Rochester Institute of Technology, School of Visual Arts, University of Cincinnati, University of Illinois, University of the Arts, University of Washington, Virginia Commonwealth University, Yale University

Chapter 4

Christine Davis, Allison Higa, Carol Finley

Chapter 8

pp. 76–77	April Greiman Inc.
pp. 78–79	Clement Mok Designs
pp. 80–81	Adobe Systems, Inc.
pp. 82–83	RGreenberg and Associates
pp. 84–85	WGBH Television
pp. 86–87	Chermayeff & Geismar, Inc.
pp. 88–89	Carbone Smolan Associates
pp. 90–91	Fitch Richardson Smith
pp. 92–93	Sussman/Prejza and Company
pp. 94–95	Doblin Group
pp. 96–97	Vignelli Associates
pp. 98–99	Ligature, Inc.
pp. 100–101	*Rolling Stone*
pp. 102–103	Milton Glaser, Inc.
pp. 104–105	Pentagram
pp. 106–107	Siegel & Gale
pp. 108–109	J. P. Morgan and Company
pp. 110–111	Walker Art Center
pp. 112–113	Richard Saul Wurman
pp. 114–115	M&Co.
pp. 116–117	Philips Electronics NV
pp. 118–119	The Sheila Studio